British History 18
The Birth of Modern

Studymates

25 Key Topics in Business Studies
25 Key Topics in Human Resources
25 Key Topics in Marketing
Accident & Emergency Nursing
British History 1870–1918
Business Organisation
Cultural Studies
English Legal System
European History 1870–1918
European Reformation
GCSE Chemistry
GCSE English
GCSE History: Schools History Project
GCSE Sciences
Genetics
Getting Started in Radio
Hitler and Nazi Germany (3rd edition)
Land Law
Lenin, Stalin and Communist Russia
Macroeconomics
Organic Chemistry
Poems To Live By
Practical Drama & Theatre Arts
Revolutionary Conflicts
Social Anthropology
Social Statistics
Speaking Better French
Speaking English
Studying Chaucer
Studying History
Studying Literature
Studying Poetry
The Changing Nature of Warfare
The New Science Teacher's Handbook
Troubleshoot Your Problems
Understanding Forces
Understanding Maths
Using Information Technology
War Poets 1914–18
Writing an Academic Essay

Many other titles in preparation

British History 1870–1918: The Birth of Modern Britain

'The Emergence of a Nation'

Robert Johnson

www.**studymates**.co.uk

© 2003 Robert Johnson

First published in 2003 by Studymates Limited, PO Box 2, Bishops Lydeard, Somerset TA3 3YE, United Kingdom

Telephone: (01823) 432002
Fax: (01823) 430097

Typeset by PDQ Typesetting, Newcastle-under-Lyme
Printed and bound in Great Britain by Bell & Bain Ltd., Glasgow

Contents

Foreword ix

Preface xi

1. The British State, Economy and Society, 1870–1900   1
One-minute summary 1
The monarchy, the government and the Establishment 1
The social classes 3
The economy 7
The 'Great Depression' and relative decline 8
Tutorial 9

2. The Reforming Ministries of Gladstone and Disraeli, 1868–1880   11
One-minute summary 11
The political situation in the 1860s 11
Liberalism and free trade 12
The reforms of Gladstone and their purpose 13
Conservatism 17
The reforms of Disraeli 19
Foreign policy 22
The Empire 26
Historical controversies 28
Tutorial 28

3. Ireland, 1868–1914   30
One-minute summary 30
The Irish question and the legacy of Union 30
Fenianism and Irish nationalism 32
The Home Rule question 34
Ulster and Unionism 36
Tutorial 38

4. The Decline of Old Certainties, 1880–1898   40
One-minute summary 40
The 'Great Depression' years 40
Gladstone's 'Ministry of Troubles' 42
Chamberlain's ideas on municipal socialism and imperialism 47
Salisbury, Randolf Churchill and Tory democracy 50
Liberal-Unionists and the decline of Liberalism 53
Conservative domination at the end of the nineteenth century 55
Tutorial 57

5. **Foreign and Imperial Policies, 1880–1902**   **59**
   One-minute summary   59
   British interests and naval power   59
   Foreign policy and the European powers: 'splendid isolation'   64
   Foreign policy 1886–1899   66
   The British Empire and new imperialism   68
   The scramble for Africa: West and East Africa   73
   The British rule in Asia   73
   The dominions   76
   The South African War, 1899–1902   77
   Tutorial   81

6. **New Liberalism, 1895–1914**   **83**
   One-minute summary   83
   The Conservatives and the 1905 election   83
   What was New Liberalism?   87
   Why was New Liberalism necessary?   88
   The reforms of New Liberalism   90
   The 1909 budget and the House of Lords dispute   93
   Old Liberalism and New Liberalism compared   97
   Tutorial   98

7. **The Crisis of Liberalism, 1910–1914**   **100**
   One-minute summary   100
   New Unionism and militant syndicalism   100
   The challenge of the suffragettes   103
   The question of Home Rule for Ireland, 1912–1914   106
   Historical controversies   108
   Tutorial   109

8. **Labour politics, 1893–1914**   **110**
   One-minute summary   110
   The origins of the Labour Party   110
   The aims of the Labour Party   111
   The significance of the Labour movement   113
   Tutorial   114

9. **Foreign Policy and International Crises, 1902–1914**   **115**
   One-minute summary   115
   The end of Britain's isolation   115
   Deterioration of relations with Germany   117
   The causes of the First World War   120
   Tutorial   122

10. **The Great War, I: 1914–1916**   **124**
    One-minute summary   124
    The Western Front, 1914–1915   124
    Attempts to break the stalemate on the Western Front   125
    Alternatives to the Western Front: the other theatres of war   127
    The British economy and the war   128
    Ireland and the Great War   130

The Battle of the Somme   132
Tutorial   135

11. The Great War, II: 1916–18   **136**
One-minute summary   136
War leadership   136
The campaigns of 1917   137
The victory of 1918   139
Interpretations of the First World War   140
Tutorial   141

12. Conclusions   **142**
One-minute summary   142
The democratisation of the State   142
Continuities in British history   143
Changes in British society   144

Glossary   146

Bibliography and further reading   147

Web sites for students   148

Index   151

List of illustrations

1. Britain's society and economy in the nineteenth and early twentieth
    centuries   6
2. Liberal and Conservative policies   16
3. Ireland: aims and methods   35
4. Foreign policy: aims and priorities   74
5. New Liberalism and Labour compared   112
6. The impact of the Great War on Britain   141

Foreword

This is a comprehensive account of a period that shaped the British twentieth century. The reader will be surprised at the number of issues that still resonate today: street violence, young offenders, New Liberalism (a forerunner of the 'third way'), constitutional reform, Ulster Unionists versus Irish Nationalists. But the key difference from our own time – the United Kingdom's status as a Great Power, with a world-wide empire – is also emphasised. Robert Johnson's text is enlivened by a discussion of those formidable politicians, W.E. Gladstone, Benjamin Disraeli, and David Lloyd George. Above all, that most profound, traumatic and revolutionary experience – the First World War – is given clear and judicious analysis. We will understand ourselves, and the world we have come from, better by reading this sensitive and informative survey.

Professor George Boyce

Preface

This Studymate guide is designed to help you acquire an understanding of the most important features of this topic as rapidly as possible. With increasing pressures on time, and with the need to read widely to obtain as many different historical opinions as you can, this guide will give you a secure knowledge of the fundamental parts of British history between 1870 and 1918. It will be, in effect, your secret weapon to success. It will draw your attention to key details, examples and evidence. It will introduce you to arguments used by historians, and the points where controversies have arisen. It will help you to progress by means of study tips and helpful advice, as well as self-test units. The format has been designed to enable to you to tackle each topic in a series of small sections, each of which is easily digestible. There is no waffle; it takes you straight to the core of the issue.

The guide is by no means exhaustive, but it will enable you to acquire the key information quickly. To assist you further, the guide also points to additional sources, reading and web sites. These will enhance your understanding, or provide you with more detail.

The format: questions, themes, sources and historiography

The guide has been designed to tackle the key questions of this era in British history, and, as such, adopts a questioning approach throughout. Many of the questions posed reflect the most common questions students face in examinations or seminars. The guide is laid out in a chronological order, but is also designed to allow you to follow a thematic path. Knowledge and use of concepts in students' work makes a considerable difference in grades achieved. Those who can grasp the overall themes of British history in this period (such as the development of democracy or the debate over private and state ownership in the British economy), and write about them, will score highly. Most important of all, the guide contains information, in summary, of historians' views and where those views conflict. An understanding and appreciation of historians' opinions will enable any student to acknowledge work which already exists in this field, and to challenge views, or obtain support for their own arguments. An ability to synthesise the debates in this period of history is the hallmark of a top candidate.

At the end of each chapter there are study tips, discussion topics and questions for you to tackle. Completion of these will enable you to check that you have understood the topic and that you really 'know' it. Document extracts will remind you of the vividness that first-hand accounts can bring to any study. You will be able to use quotes from these in your work. Critical analysis of documents is a vital skill for the historian and the source-based questions will help you to master this craft.

Robert Johnson

The British State, Economy and Society, 1870–1900

One-minute summary – In 1870, Great Britain was the world's leading industrial power with an Empire that spanned the globe. Her production of coal, iron and steel exceeded that of any other country. She possessed a vast merchant fleet with which to import raw materials and export the finished products. This fleet and its sea lanes were protected by the formidable Royal Navy. In addition, London was the world's financial capital and the administrative centre for banking, insurance and investment. Her currency was backed by the gold standard. Politically, Britain had made significant progress towards a full democracy. After 1867, some working men of modest means had the right to vote. This led to the greater intervention of the state in society, for the British people demanded improvements to living and working conditions. However, it was still a nation of great contrasts. By the end of the nineteenth century, social surveys revealed that a third of the British public lived at or below the poverty line. The aristocracy, who had dominated politics for centuries, continued to exercise considerable influence in government. Between them stood the middling classes whose ideas and fashions shaped much of the culture of late-nineteenth century Britain. However, above all, this was a period of change. Every aspect of British life was touched by the effects of industrialisation and political change. Externally, the balance of power was also shifting. Europe and North America began to challenge British industrial and commercial hegemony. British society in 1900 was very different indeed from that of 1870.

In this chapter you will learn:

▶ the organisation of the British state
▶ the classes and strata of British society
▶ the economic background to Britain's 'take-off' period and relative decline.

The monarchy, the government and the Establishment

The monarchy was the apex of the constitution and state

Queen Victoria was Britain's longest reigning monarch. She was crowned in 1837 and died 63 years later in 1901. Although head of state, Victoria actually possessed very little constitutional power. She had to give her assent to parliamentary decisions, and she freely offered her opinions throughout her reign, but real power rested with Parliament. Nevertheless, she was treated with great respect and was kept informed of all government business. Victoria suffered a deep personal loss with her death of her husband Albert in 1861, and her withdrawal from public life did much to erode the popularity which Albert had built up for the monarchy. However, her longevity seemed to represent the stability of Britain and the jubilee celebrations of 1887 and 1897 witnessed genuine outpourings of public appreciation. By contrast, republicanism in Britain was virtually unknown. Only in Ireland, where other grievances coincided, did any anti-monarchical feeling become public.

The government of Britain was a system of checks and balances

The British political system was a complex balance of power which had emerged over many centuries. At its core in 1870 was the sovereignty of Parliament. The two chambers, of Commons and Lords, had won concessions from the British monarchy from the sixteenth century onwards. In the mid-nineteenth century, a government was formed by either peers from the House of Lords or members of the House of Commons, who affiliated themselves to a political party. Groups of MPs (Members of Parliament from the Commons) formed parties based on shared interests, but they tended to be fluid organisations until the mid-nineteenth century. The party in power had to canvass the voters for a mandate (permission) to govern for a period of five to seven years through the process known as a general election. A select group of the victorious party, called the Cabinet, met to decide on policy. The party that lost the election formed the Opposition. Its role was to challenge government policy and debate the issues of the day with the government in the Commons. All policies were presented as Bills to the two Houses where they were debated and voted upon, the greatest number of votes carrying the Bill forward. Once the Bill had undergone three readings (and debates) in the Commons, and then a further three readings in the Lords, it was given royal assent and became an Act of Parliament. It was then recorded on the Statute Books and implemented by a bureaucracy called the Civil Service.

The legal system was independent and the constitution was flexible

The processes of passing laws, and the checks and balances in power, were enshrined in the British constitution. This was not a written document, unlike in America. Instead, it worked on the basis of 'precedent'. Previous practice provided the benchmark of procedure and conduct, yet the unwritten aspect meant that it had great flexibility: it could meet the inevitability of change and adapt, but preserve continuity and stability.

The judiciary (the body concerned with the supervision of British laws) was entirely independent of the polity (the political decision-making body). This ensured that corruption was minimised. Corruption was also kept at bay by the values which politicians brought from their class background.

The social classes

The aristocracy was small in number but influential

The aristocracy was the titled nobility who had, in feudal times, provided the monarch's closest and richest retainers. They were distinctive in their land ownership and they were traditionally dependent on their income from the land (farming and rents). In his excellent study, *The Decline and Fall of the British Aristocracy*, Professor Cannadine identified three subdivisions in the land owners of Britain. In 1870, about 6,000 families could be classed as small landowners, holding between 1,000 and 10,000 acres with rental incomes of between £1,000 and £10,000 a year. County squires, full-time landowners and 'rentiers' could all fall into this category. The second group (of 750 families) held between 10,000 and 30,000 acres either scattered across the country or consolidated in one county, and they enjoyed rental incomes up to £30,000 a year. This group was distinct from the middle classes, or the lesser landowners, by the wealth and scale of this ownership. The third group consisted of 250 families whose holdings often straddled counties and whose incomes were frequently derived from non-agricultural sources. The super-rich had the capital available from the beginning of the industrial revolution to invest in, and therefore exploit the development that subsequently took place.

The powers of the Establishment were historically in the hands of the aristocracy

The aristocracy were also the political élite. In 1880 there were 580 peers (431 of whom held their titles on an hereditary basis) in the House of Lords. This upper chamber wielded considerable power. It could amend or reject any Bill from the Commons, except money bills (such as the annual budget submitted by the Chancellor of the Exchequer). Just as important were family ties. Many of the Lords were related to members of the various Cabinets, or served in them themselves. The network continued downwards from Parliament. Below the titled nobility there were 856 Baronets (hereditary knighthood) who became virtually indistinguishable from the peerage. Below this group a further 4,250 names were listed in the contemporary register, *Burkes Peerage*, as members of this august association. The judiciary, the officer corps of the army, the church and the civil service were dominated by sons of the gentry. Cannadine concluded that: 'The members of the titled and genteel classes were not merely the lords of the earth, they were also the stars of the firmament. They boasted unrivalled and unquestioned glamour and prestige'.

The political situation was changing by 1900

Traditionally, the franchise (right to vote) had been restricted to those with considerable wealth in property. The 1832 Great Reform Act had removed the monopoly of rule by the aristocracy by extending the franchise and lowering the property qualification to vote or stand for parliament. (This applied to those who held property or paid rent to a value of £10 a year in the towns or £50 in the counties.) The 'new wealth' of manufacturers and the middle class began to share power. By 1865, despite a rise in population and growth of industrial towns, only one million (out of five million) adult males had the vote. The aristocrats continued to dominate party membership and political leadership. In the 1860s it was claimed that one third of the House of Commons was filled by no more than 60 families, all landed. Three-quarters of them were patricians (aristocrats). The dominance was self-perpetuating; the hegemony of the aristocracy seemed to be the natural order of things. It represented and reinforced the idea of hierarchy in society as a whole. However, radical (left wing) spokesmen began to question the power of the Lords. Henry Labouchere tabled a motion in the 1880s calling for a readjustment in the relative powers of the two chambers. In 1910, Lloyd George initiated an election campaign against the Lords called 'Peers versus the people'.

The aristocracy were not unpopular
The values of the aristocracy tended to influence the rest of society. A sense of public duty ran through them, inspiring the middle class to emulate them, and propelling hundreds of lesser noblemen into the service of ruling and running the British Empire. Aristocrats were sought as patrons and honourable presidents to lend a degree of prestige to companies, organisations and charitable work. In addition, the leisure pursuits of country life – hunting, shooting, fishing and racing were popularised by the spread of leisure activities across British society. The power of the House of Lords was not challenged until 1910 because it fulfilled a vital function. It tempered the legislation of the Commons (whose Bills might be presented, not for the good of the country, but for the benefit of their own party interests) and debated it in a cooler and more considered way. The Lords tended to test legislation with a simple formula: was it the best for the crown, the constitution and the country?

The middle classes were an important and expanding layer of society
Despite the tendency to see the middle class as one strata of society, the contemporary notion of calling them *classes* was probably more accurate. Class is often poorly defined for it includes more than a division of society by wealth. Employment, values, and the independence of their means might also be relevant. The middle classes were a broad group by 1870, including the professions, businessmen, bankers, shop owners and manufacturers. By 1900, there was even greater diversity. Clerks, staff of financial services, small-scale lawyers in provincial towns, retailers, men in advertising, journalists and small traders might all fall into the category of lower middle class. The vast legions of small-scale businesses and manufacturers, and the growth of the service sector in the economy, and the fact that they voted (where many of the working class still did not) meant that this 'class' was of considerable importance in the period 1870–1918. The steady rise of wages in these sectors fuelled the aspirations of the lower middle class and gave a great impetus to the consumerisation of the economy.

They purchased their own terraced or semi-detached houses in the new suburbs which expanded rapidly around all of Britain's cities. They often commuted to the city centres on the branch lines of the railways. Suburbia, with neat gardens in front of every property, brought the countryside into the city. This combined the advantages of urban life with the ethos of luxury associated with the aristocracy who lived in the countryside.

Middle-class or Victorian values were pervasive

The middle classes exuded confidence throughout the nineteenth century. They valued enterprise and individualism which were the hallmarks of liberalism. They valued promotion on merit as a reward for industry and efficiency. Yet they maintained their differences from the working class in this respect by a belief in competition, in the value of property, and, above all, by respectability. This took various forms, but was manifest in strict obedience to rules of behaviour and etiquette, respect for hierarchy and a deep sense of duty, purpose and religious conviction. In many towns, the middle classes developed a strong civic pride. In Birmingham, for example, Joseph Chamberlain and his supporters carried out a wide range of public works, removing slums, erecting public buildings, providing street lighting or developing an efficient clean water supply and sewerage systems. Few towns were without a rifle volunteer detachment, or a bandstand and public park, in the 1890s. Victorian values are deeply etched into British society, not least because they became the guiding ethos for many public (that is, private) schools. Young men were groomed by strict adherence to their principles in order to fit them for the challenge of government, management, or imperial rule.

The middle classes also stimulated the growth of the popular press

The Times, which had risen to prominence in the 1840s, remained 'high brow' reading, but the *Daily Mail*, founded in 1896, often replaced provincial papers in popularity ratings. The modern format of political, sporting and perhaps scandalous news was quickly established. There was a considerable appetite for the exotic and dramatic. Newspapers were always politically orientated, but the *Mail* reflected a transfer of allegiance by the lower middle class at the end of the nineteenth century; it began as a liberal-imperialist organ, and became Unionist-Conservative by 1900. The reasons for this can be found in Chapter 4. Newspaper articles are an excellent source for historians, retaining as they do the vividness and immediacy of contemporary issues, and embellished with editorials designed to appeal to middle-class tastes.

The working classes were as stratified as the middle classes

The working classes were as diverse as the middle classes and it is somewhat misleading to think of them as an homogenous group. There were distinct regional variations, religious denominations, employment patterns and local customs. Those in regular, skilled work with higher wages have been identified as the 'aristocracy of labour'. They tended to be organised in trade unions, moderate in

Population (millions)

1871 census	1891 census	1901 census	1911 census
31.4	37.7	41.5	45.2

Employment in Industries (millions)

	1871	1901	1931
Agriculture	1.8	1.5	1.3
Mining	0.6	0.9	1.2
Manufacturing	3.9	5.5	7.2
Construction	0.8	1.3	1.1

Balance of Payments

	Imports	Exports /Re-exports	Overseas investment earnings	trade	Invisible Balance
1900	523.1	291/63.2	103.6	109.1	37.9
1910	678.3	430.4/103.8	170	146.7	167.3
1920	1,932	1,334/222.8	200	395	252

Steel Production (as a percentage of world production)

	United Kingdom	USA	Germany
1875–79	35.9	26	16.6
1890–94	24.6	33.7	21.4

Fig. 1. Britain's society and economy in the nineteenth and early twentieth centuries.

their politics and eminently respectable. After the introduction of compulsory education in 1870, they became increasingly literate. At the lower end of the working classes, workers might be less skilled and therefore more likely to be laid off (become unemployed). Their wages would certainly be lower. These men tended to look to the upper working class for leadership, but towards the end of the century they began to organise themselves into their own trade unions. Their political outlook tended to be more radical, but employers usually had the upper hand in disputes. Nevertheless, wages improved for all those in employment throughout the second half of the nineteenth century. Between 1880 and 1896, real wages increased by 45%. Smaller families (compared with the previous century) gave greater spending power to the family unit. In addition, more leisure time became available.

The poor lived a life of hardship at the turn of the century
Charles Booth's social survey of 1889, although containing many errors and subjective judgements, has proved to be a valuable source for historians. Booth identified a range of five categories of people in London. A much smaller group than the 'regular standard earnings', which typified the working class, was the poor. Booth believed these people were either intermittently or casually employed, or belonged to the 'lowest class'. There could be movement between categories and some could 'get on', but life for those at or below the poverty line

was hard by any standard. Basic needs of food and shelter were the main preoccupation. With no provision for sickness or injury at work, these tragedies could condemn a person to a life of particular hardship. Many working-class people feared that they might have to spend their final years in the workhouse; the ultimate indignity. Some of the poor picked up work when they could, a few turned to crime, and women who couldn't get jobs as domestic servants, as 'maids of all work', might turn to prostitution. Their dwellings were often of the lowest quality, with several generations of the family sharing a room or two. The poor were also under-nourished. Dockers who went on strike in 1889 drew attention to their meagre diet during their protests; thin soup augmented with fish heads.

Despite hardship, the lower classes enjoyed a culture of their own

Working-class culture was a diverse mix of regionalism, religious affinities and respectability. Watching football, a sport that became professional by the 1880s, was an expression of solidarity and an extension of civic pride. Some teams from the same city were formed on sectarian lines (Celtic was Catholic and Rangers Protestant in Glasgow). Money was spared not just for the entrance fee or away match, but also for betting too. Horses, dogs, and eventually football pools offered just the chance of escaping poverty in one fell swoop. However, as Robert Roberts observed in *The Classic Slum: Salford Life in the First Quarter of the Century* (1971), the 'fastest way out of Manchester' was to get drunk. Roberts also recalled how teenagers amongst the poor fought street battles. He wrote: 'Deprived of all decent ways of spending their little leisure, they sought escape from tedium in bloody battles with belt and clog...This form of violence, vicious and purposeless, seemed to have its root in a subconscious wish to establish "territory". Not only children but adults too felt that the street where they dwelt was in some way their private property'.

The economy

The industrial revolution changed Britain

From the mid-eighteenth century, Britain was transformed by the industrial revolution. The coincidence of abundant foodstuffs, mineral resources, a vast labour force and the invention of new technologies produced a rapid growth in the economy. Mass production ensured goods could be made more rapidly and more cheaply. Railways supplied raw materials and distributed finished goods to the domestic market (particularly the expanding cities) and to the ports for export. Between 1850 and 1873, the economy grew at a rate of 3% per year. The value of cotton exports rose from £46 million in 1851 to £105 million. Steam power was also applied to shipping, reducing travel times and cutting costs. Production increased in the extraction industries. Coal was mined to a total of 65 million tonnes a year in 1855, and increased to 110 million tonnes in 1870. By 1900, it had reached a total of 225 million tonnes. This was the 'take-off' period of the industrial revolution.

Industrialisation had a major impact on British life

In 1851, for the first time, more people lived in urban areas than in the countryside. By 1900, 80% of Britons were urban-dwellers. Part of this growth can be explained by the rise in population (as the death rate fell) and also by the changes in agriculture which reduced the demand for labour in that sector. Most people rented their accommodation but the quality of housing varied enormously. Well planned, or affluent areas, stood in juxtaposition with old zones, slums and poorly constructed terraces built by opportunists. New working conditions were imposed on the British people to maximise efficiency too. Time itself was altered. Local time zones across Britain were abolished by the arrival of the railways. Time discipline was enforced and shift work introduced in some factories. In 1850, 596,000 people worked in these regulated factories. By 1900, that figure had risen to 1.1 million. In one hundred years, the landscape of Britain was altered from an exclusively agrarian vista, to an urbanised and industrialised land. Its population was released from the bonds of subsistence, and, as a consumer society, was dependent on the production and distribution of the new economy.

The 'Great Depression' and relative decline

Was there a 'Great Depression' 1873–94?

There has been disagreement among historians as to the nature and extent of a depression, or economic downturn, in the period 1873–1894. R.A. Church argued that there was indeed a depression in the British economy. After the boom of the mid-Victorian era, the imposition of tariffs by Italy (1878), Germany (1879), France (1882) and America (1883), and the competition from their industries, led to a reduction in demand for British goods. This led to unemployment amongst British workers: from 1% of the workforce in 1872 to 11.4% in 1879. The economy (in terms of industrial production) continued to grow, but at a much reduced rate. The rate of growth in Germany (unified as a nation state in 1871) and the United States (with the opening up of the prairies and the exploitation of her mineral wealth) seemed to suggest that, in time, other countries would catch up with Britain's lead and even surpass it. Manufacturers expressed concern that prices, and therefore profits, were falling. Lord Randolph Churchill felt that Britain's trade was affected by a 'mortal disease'. The optimism of the 1850s had gone.

The situation was not as bleak as contemporaries feared

S.B. Saul wrote, in *The Myth of the Great Depression* (1969), that the pessimism of the 1870s was exaggerated. The British economy continued to grow throughout the period, and Britain was still perhaps the world's leading industrial power in 1900. Coal production increased by 23.5% in the 1880s alone. Although Britain's share of the world steel market was getting smaller, it would have shrunk anyway since Britain had been virtually the only steel producer at first, and, as other countries developed this technology, it was inevitable that Britain's lead would be eroded.

In other words, Britain's steel industry was not in decline, but booming. Although there was unemployment, falling prices actually helped the consumer. As wages increased throughout this period, the spending power of the working classes increased and this in turn stimulated industry with greater consumer demand. S.B. Saul argued that the rest of the world also suffered a loss of business confidence and slow down in their economies; this is the very reason why countries like Germany and America imposed tariffs. They wanted to protect their own industries against foreign competition. In conclusion, Saul refuted the idea that there had been a 'depression' between 1873 and 1894.

There was a relative decline in British industry
Although there was no absolute decline in Britain's production, or the value of her exports, the speed at which Germany and the USA were catching up with Britain was a cause for concern. In 1900, both of these countries produced more steel and more coal. Whilst this was inevitable, given their greater natural resources and larger domestic market, British exports of finished manufactures also declined, and Britain exported more machinery, coal and ships. These were the products, backed by investment capital from the City of London (the financial centre), which would enable other countries to compete with Britain. Britain therefore faced a future of greater competition, and unfavourable trends of growth compared with other industrial powers.

Tutorial

Progress questions
1. Why did the aristocracy remain so dominant in British politics between 1870 and 1900?

2. In what ways could the House of Lords modify the policies of elected governments?

3. What was Joseph Chamberlain famous for in the 1870s and 1880s?

4. In what ways were middle-class and working-class values different?

5. What do you understand by the following: 'By 1900, Britain's economy was in relative decline'.

Seminar discussion
1. How could the House of Lords protect the constitution?

2. To what extent did Britain suffer a 'Great Depression' between 1873–1894?

Practical assignment
Examine the sources. What defined class in late Victorian Britain? Using the sources explain how class barriers were maintained.

O.B. Bunce, *Don't: A Manual of Mistakes and Improprieties more or less prevalent in Conduct and Speech* (1886) pp. 12–13.

Don't tuck your napkin under your chin, or spread it upon your breast. Bibs
and tuckers are for the nursery. Don't spread your napkin over your lap;
let it fall over your knee.
Don't gurgle, or draw in your breath, or make other noises from eating soup.
Don't ask for a second service of soup.
Don't bite your bread. Break it off. Don't break your bread into your soup.
Don't use a steel knife with fish. A silver knife is now placed by the side of each
plate for the fish course.
Don't eat vegetables with a spoon. Eat them with a fork...

Flora Thompson, *Lark Rise, an Oxfordshire hamlet in the 'eighties* (1939) p. 17.

Good manners prevailed. The children were given their share of the food,
there was no picking and choosing, and they were expected to eat in silence.
'Please' and 'Thank you' were permitted, but nothing more. ... Father might
shovel green peas into his mouth with his knife, Mother might drink tea from
her saucer and some of the children might lick their plates when their food
was devoured; but who could eat peas with a two pronged fork, or wait for tea
to cool after the heat and flurry of cooking, and licking plates passed as a
graceful compliment to Mother's good dinner.

Study tips

1. Make a list of the values of the aristocracy, middle classes and the working
classes to get a feel for how British society worked.

2. Try to remember the significance and importance of the industrial revolution
throughout this study. Shifts in the economy could have a direct and
dramatic impact on other areas of British life.

3. Try to remember a few key figures in the statistical data offered in this
chapter. Being able to use them in your work lends a degree of accuracy and
empiricism (reference to evidence) which is impressive.

4. Make a note of key events and personalities which appear briefly in this
chapter. Notes help you to retain information that you have read. They also
help you to focus on the most vital information. Review them periodically
and remind yourself to do so with a diary entry.

2

The Reforming Ministries of Gladstone and Disraeli, 1868–1880

One-minute summary – The period between 1868 and 1880 was one of great change. Divided by personal animosity as well as different policies, the Victorian Prime Ministers Gladstone and Disraeli seemed equally determined to effect changes in British society and the political system. They shared a belief though, that the economy was beyond government interference. Free trade and the benefits of capitalist economic development were unquestioned. As leaders, these two men shaped and dominated the ethos of their parties. Gladstone represented sobriety, respectability, and the promotion of equality of opportunity for the individual. He aimed to preserve peace, minimise government expenditure and reform the 'proved abuses' of society. Disraeli, by contrast, reflected enterprise, opportunism and patriotism. He was prepared to risk war and use any measure to preserve the establishment. These differences led to considerable improvements for the working classes and greater opportunities in the administration for the middle classes. However, both lost elections because their policies failed to sustain support amongst the electorate.

In this chapter you will learn about:

▶ the political situation in the 1860s
▶ Liberalism and free trade
▶ the reforms of Gladstone and their purpose
▶ Conservatism
▶ the reforms of Disraeli
▶ foreign policy 1868–1880
▶ the Empire
▶ historical controversies.

The political situation in the 1860s

The Conservatives had been out of office since 1846 with the exception of some minority governments. The governments of the period were usually coalitions of other interests, broadly united by the concept of free trade and *laissez faire* (non-intervention) in other aspects of government. However, in 1866 a radical Reform Bill was presented to Parliament proposing to enfranchise the working classes. Progress towards this Bill had been initiated by extra-parliamentary pressure groups such as Robert Applegarth's trade union colleagues, the Reform Union (1864) and the radical orator John Bright. William Gladstone, a Chancellor of the

Exchequer who had done much to move Britain towards free trade by abolishing tariffs, declared that he felt 'Every man ... is morally entitled to come within the pale of the constitution.' The radicals' Bill was defeated, and the Liberal coalition leader, Lord Russell resigned. A Conservative government thus found itself faced with public agitation for reform. A poor harvest, a cholera epidemic in London and rioting at Hyde Park convinced Lord Derby and his leader in the Commons, Disraeli, to introduce a bill more radical than the liberal one and thus steal any support their opponents might have gained. This was nicknamed 'Dishing the Whigs'.

The 1867 Reform Act and its significance
No one knew exactly how the new working-class electorate would vote, so the Act was a 'leap in the dark'. Some Conservative Cabinet members resigned. There was widespread concern that these uneducated working-class men would be a 'horde of selfish and obscure mediocrities, incapable of anything but mischief' (Disraeli). Some feared that they would be prey to bribery because of their 'venality, ignorance, drunkenness and facility for being intimidated' (Robert Lowe). Voters now totalled 2.46 million, but the south and east was better represented than the north. Rural labourers still couldn't vote and a public ballot meant that intimidation could not be ruled out. In larger constituencies it would be harder to 'treat' all the voters so politicians began to appeal to the sentiments of the new electorate. Equally, the drawing of electoral boundaries could make a difference to the number of votes for candidates. Local organisations were developed to maximise voter support. Thus the idea of popular politics was born in the first fledgling democracy.

Liberalism and free trade

Liberalism
Liberalism was the broad political philosophy that held together the various elements that made up the Liberal Party, namely the Whigs (aristocratic reformers), the Peelites (those who subscribed to the ideas of the 1840s reformer Sir Robert Peel), and the radicals (the progression reformers). Liberals believed in respect for the rights of the individual and their property. They were in favour of the reform of 'proved abuses' in society and wanted to see the preservation of peace, believing that war was both costly and immoral. A strong religious conviction drove many Liberals, and from the 1880s, Liberal support came from the 'Celtic fringe' of Cornwall and the South-West of England, Wales, Scotland and Ireland. The Liberals were the party of choice of many manufacturers until the 1880s, but also of many urban workers. However, D.A. Hamer and Martin Pugh have referred to the survival of serious divisions in the Liberal Party. Only Gladstone's leadership held the Party together.

Free trade
Free trade was more than a demand for the abolition of tariffs on imports and exports, although this was its main thrust in the mid-nineteenth century. Free trade also meant the fostering of reciprocal arrangements in other countries which might reduce international rivalry and preserve peace. It also meant freedom from state interference. John Stuart Mill (*Principles of Political Economy*, 1848) wrote that the intervention of the state should be minimised. Every individual should create wealth through his own enterprise. 'Self-help' was a popular expression of the 1860s. Economists who observed Britain's 'take-off' in the mid-century felt that the world would follow the British model. There was a sense of inevitability about Britain's progress and a sense of optimism prevailed for decades. It even affected the work of intellectuals. Charles Darwin's *On the Origin of Species* (1859), which expounded the concept of evolution, reflected the spirit of the age, despite the profound shock expressed when Darwin revealed that humankind and the apes share a common ancestry. This was wrongly interpreted to suggest that man is descended from apes, in fact they are our cousins and not our Grandparents. Evolution was a positivistic idea (it offered an explanation of the past and a set of laws that could explain the future) and it matched the idea that governments should avoid interfering with the laws of nature, be they economic or social.

The reforms of Gladstone and their purpose

Gladstone aimed to tackle the issues of the time
It is vital to understand what the grievances were that Gladstone felt compelled to change. In summary they were:

▶ The continuing privilege of the aristocracy and upper middle classes in education, government and administration.

▶ Poor housing, health, sanitation, water supply, standards of food hygiene, and conditions of employment for the working classes.

▶ Education was not available to all, but the churches provided what they could for the poorer in society.

▶ There was no support for those who were sick, infirm, or out of work.

▶ Child labour was still common.

▶ The state possessed no sources of information on the conditions of the two thirds of society who could be classed as working class or poor, other than the observations of a handful of intellectuals.

Gladstone's first ministry (1868–1874): significance
The most significant aspects of this ministry were two-fold. First, it defined liberalism as a reforming credo that relied on Gladstone's own interests and

personality. Second, it demonstrated that Gladstone's aspirations were difficult to fulfil in practice. The Liberals also advocated retrenchment (minimising government expenditure), peace in their foreign policy and reform.

Gladstone's reforms

E.J. Feuchtwanger argues that the reforms of this ministry were significant because they largely '*defined* liberalism in this period'. Michael Bentley (*The Climax of Liberal Politics*, 1987) believed that this ministry was 'one of the most energetic and prolific administrations of the nineteenth century'. The reforms covered:

▶ Abolition of compulsory church rates.

▶ Abolition of exclusions to Catholics and Nonconformists at Oxford and Cambridge universities under the University Tests Act 1871.

▶ Abolition of Purchase (where men could simply buy commissions in the army even if they had no aptitude). The reform caused so much anger in the Lords that it was introduced by Royal Warrant, not as an Act of Parliament.

▶ The Enlistment Act reduced the time of service in the army to three years if preferred, and the Regulation Act increased the size of the army. These military reforms were the work of Edward Cardwell.

▶ The establishment of free, compulsory, primary education (1870) either under church control, as before, or as the new locally funded Board Schools. This legislation was organised by W.E. Forster.

▶ The establishment of competitive entrance examinations for the civil service (thus opening this role to the middle classes) in 1870.

▶ The introduction of a secret ballot in 1872 (to avoid intimidation at elections).

▶ The Public Health Act 1872 established urban sanitation boards and a Local Government Act brought responsibilities for health under a local government authority.

▶ The Judicature Act 1873 reorganised and rationalised the court system.

▶ The Licensing Act 1872 restricted opening hours largely on the urgings of temperance pressure groups, but it was designed to combat absenteeism from work through over-drinking.

▶ The Trade Union Act 1871 gave legal recognition to the New Model [Trades] Unions, but the Criminal Law Amendment Act 1871 made intimidation during strikes illegal. Whilst this was designed to fulfil the liberal principle of protecting the individual, the Gas Stokers Case of 1872 demonstrated that the judges could interpret virtually any picketing as intimidatory. Faced with the prospect of criminal charges, the unions realised that strike action would be hazardous.

▶ There were also reforms in Ireland, namely, the Disestablishment of the Church of Ireland (1869) and the Land Act (1870). (See Chapter 3.)

The reforms seemed to herald a great change in British society
Taken together the reforms seemed to represent an attack on the privileges of the few. The Church of England had lost its supremacy in education, particularly at the universities. The House of Lords had delayed a few bills but had accepted reform of the law lords in the Judicature Act (1873). The aristocracy no longer monopolised the civil service or the army's officer corps.

There were several reasons for opposition to the reforms
Britain was the leading manufacturing nation in the world. In other words, in the 1860s most of the world's man-made products came from Britain. No one wanted to ruin this arrangement. Britain's society and constitution gave the most power and responsibility to those who were educated and 'fit' to govern. It seemed absurd to give responsibility for Britain's foreign policy to a labourer from the streets. Opposition also came from the Liberal Party's radicals. Radicals had a reputation (which was often unfair) for opposing monarchs, opposing the constitution, supporting the worst atrocities of the French Revolution, agitating and fomenting unrest amongst workers, and generally propagating ideas against capital and property. The sheer volume of reforms alarmed some of the middle classes. There were other sources of opposition: the Irish were dissatisfied with the land reforms (see Chapter 3), the trade unions felt that strikes were virtually impossible, brewers and publicans were angry at the licensing reform and they transferred their allegiance *en masse* to the Conservatives, and anti-drinking lobbyists were dissatisfied; they felt the licensing reform didn't go far enough. From the established institutions, aristocratic army officers, including the Commander in Chief, the Duke of Cambridge, disliked Cardwell's reforms (he was suspicious of all 'Pwogress') and the churches were dissatisfied with the creation of secular schools.

Verdict on Gladstone's reforms: defeat in the 1874 election
Most historians, such as Philip Magnus, would say that Gladstone's efforts were to be applauded, but that his ideas were either flawed or inadequate. Gladstone seems to have been motivated by a genuine desire to carry out a Christian duty of helping the less fortunate, but he was still a Victorian, with ideas that poverty was in part caused by indolence (a sin) or other vices. Order, prosperity, prudence in expenditure, the protection of property, and the reform of 'proved abuses' by established institutions were Victorian liberal ideals. These ranked alongside the more familiar ideas of liberty and the protection of the rights of the individual, and of property, manifest in the Criminal Law Amendment Act. The most

Policy	Liberals	Conservatives
Monarchy and privilege	To reduce the power of the small élite whilst showing respect for the monarchy and reforming in a moderate way.	To preserve the monarchy and the constitutional arrangements as they were. Strong feeling that reform had gone far enough.
The middle classes	Gladstone appealed to a strong sense of morality and respectability. Liberals aimed to open up all institutions and positions of power to the middle classes.	The Conservatives hoped to appeal to the patriotism and class prejudice against the lower classes by the middle classes. They stressed their support for property and respectability.
The workers	The Liberals hoped to make improvements in the workplace.	The Conservatives meant to uphold the interests of employers, but could see the benefit of winning the sympathy of the workers too.
Schools and health	Increasingly the Liberals came to see the need to improve education and health for all classes and for Gladstone it was a Christian mission.	The poor did not feature in Conservative thinking, except that their faith in a booming economy was believed to benefit everyone in society eventually as wealth would trickle down to all.
Foreign policy	The Liberals aimed to preserve peace and promote British trade. This meant being conciliatory at times but each case was to be judged on its merits.	The Conservatives could see that unless Britain was prepared to defend its interests other powers would seek to replace Britain's pre-eminent world position.

Fig. 2. Liberal and Conservative policies.

damaging reform was the trade union legislation, even though Gladstone thought the Licensing Act was the most damaging. He exclaimed, when defeated in the general election of 1874: 'We have been borne down in a torrent of gin and beer'. This shows how he judged everything in moral terms, but he didn't acknowledge the wider impact of his reforms. It should also be noted that there were other contributory factors in his defeat in 1874. These were the attacks by the Conservative opposition, his foreign policy, and the divisions in his own Party.

The effect of Conservative opposition cannot be discounted
Disraeli, the leader of the Conservatives from 1868, launched a vitriolic attack on Gladstone as leader of the Liberal Party. He described him as a 'half-mad firebrand', and sarcastically as a 'sophisticated rhetorician inebriated with the exuberance of his own verbosity'. Where Gladstone was a measured but verbose speaker, Disraeli was witty and quick. In April 1872, conscious that the reforming zeal of the Liberal Party was on the wane, Disraeli observed: 'As I sat opposite the Treasury Bench, the Ministers reminded me of one of those marine landscapes not very unusual on the coasts of South America. You behold a range of exhausted volcanoes. Not a single flame flickers on a single pallid crest'. These attacks were memorable and did much damage to Gladstone's image.

Divisions in the Liberal Party added to their weakness
The Party divisions began to emerge as the first batch of reforms had been passed. Although the Tories would have opposed the Liberals anyway, the Nonconformists had supported the radicals in British politics and should have been behind Gladstone. They were dissatisfied by the speed of progress against the Establishment. Yet by 1872, there was concern amongst the Whigs of the party that a radical programme had been passed and that the government shouldn't go too far. Despite the division in the Party, the electorate were not yet voting on entrenched class lines. Those that could vote were open to persuasion by effective public speeches, newspaper reports and their friends, families, employers and colleagues.

Gladstone's foreign policy appeared weak
The Liberal foreign policy seemed to show weakness, and was in contrast to the previous Whig Prime Minister, Lord Palmerston, who had taken a belligerent and nationalist line in almost all of his policies. When the Franco-Prussian War broke out in Europe, there was a danger that Belgium would be invaded. Britain was pledged to protect this country and would have had to enter the conflict if either the German or French forces had crossed the Belgian frontier. Gladstone swiftly negotiated the guarantee of Belgian neutrality, but in doing so effectively endorsed whichever side won as the hegemonic power on the continent. Gladstone also seemed to give way to easily to Russian demands at the end of the Franco-Prussian War. Russia had been barred from putting a fleet on the Black Sea after the joint Anglo-French expedition to the Crimea in 1854–56. When France was defeated in the Franco-Prussian War, Russia knew that Britain would be unable to enforce its regulation of the Black Sea on its own. The Russian navy therefore occupied the Black Sea and Gladstone was presented with a *fait accompli*. To preserve British prestige, he called a conference at London and formally conceded to Russian interests.

Gladstone awarded the USA compensation which was unpopular in Britain
The American government claimed compensation for the damage done by British ships in the service of the southern states during the American Civil War (1861–65). Gladstone agreed to pay the USA £3.25 million in 1872, but it was deeply unpopular in Britain. A Conservative back-bencher remarked that the Liberals had a 'strange mania for eating dirt'.

Conservatism

What was Conservatism?
Modern Conservatism emerged through adaptation to changing circumstances. Each leader of the party has redefined its position. Since the 1980s there has been a shift from Thatcherite Conservatism (a highly centralised state, but free market

forces), to Majorism (a reluctance to embrace Europe, a foreign policy in support of the USA and a less overt freedom in the economy but with continued privatisation of state industries and utilities) to a new brand of Conservatism under Michael Howard's leadership, via William Hague and Iain Duncan Smith. However, the central points of Conservatism in the broadest sense, for the period 1870–1918, are identifiable. These included:

▶ *Support for the monarchy.* Its maintenance was seen as the central element of a hub of patronage and honours, the continuance of the United Kingdom as an independent state, the promotion of British trade, and the crown of national prestige.

▶ *Support for the established institutions.* These were regarded as moderating influences in a political environment otherwise swayed by the emotions of the masses and the media. The Judges, the Lords, the gentry, the (upper) middle classes, the rural set and the London social set preserved their influence in powerful lobbies against the progressive forces of the other parties.

▶ *Promotion of law and order.* This was vital in a society threatened by anarchy. The aim was to preserve property, life and limb. Wrongdoers were to be punished as much as 'reformed'.

▶ *Freedom in the economy.* Freedom of enterprise, free market forces and private property were the hallmark of Conservative economics. They were the ultimate capitalist party. This changed after the First World War because of the need to protect the more vulnerable in society, but it could be argued that Disraeli took a more interventionist line in the 1870s.

▶ *Patriotism.* Usually expressed through genteel sentimentality towards the mother country although strong passions could be aroused when national interests were threatened. Rarely expressed as nationalism, and too respectable to be racist, (although a few persisted in prejudice), patriotism compelled men to serve a greater cause than their own self-interests. For example, efforts to improve the life of imperial subjects was regarded as a national duty.

▶ *Support for the Church of England.* Christianity was universally accepted by the Conservatives, fitting in with the concept of doing 'good works'. The Church of England has long supported the monarchy which in turn promised to be the defender of the faith. A deep sense of moral and physical duty developed organically out of this association with the Church.

▶ *Reform in an 'Even and friendly temper'* (Sir Robert Peel's promise of 1834). Reform was usually moderate, uncontroversial, and, after 1900, accepted that the state had a duty to protect the weak. Until then, the Conservative view of reform was to create the conditions for 'self-help', that is, the usual

Victorian idea of self-improvement. State intervention was viewed with suspicion until then. However, even after 1900, reform of the 'Established Institutions' was rarely considered beneficial; the emphasis was on continuity and tradition.

The reforms of Disraeli

The new philosophy of Conservatism was announced by Sir Robert Peel at Tamworth (December 1834) and it acknowledged that, after the 1832 Reform Act, changes to the political system were inevitable. There was a further change in 1846 with the Repeal of the Corn Laws which marked the beginning of an era of free trade. At first there was opposition to this economic reform, and one of the chief critics was Benjamin Disraeli. He attacked Sir Robert Peel for betraying the interests of his own party, namely to protect the interests of the aristocracy and middle classes against the radicals. However, the Conservatives, or Tories (as Disraeli continued to call them), were only able to form minority governments or coalitions under Lord Aberdeen or Lord Derby. Then, in 1867, Disraeli and Derby triumphed by passing the Second Parliamentary Reform Act. This brilliant opportunism nevertheless proved short-lived. Disraeli lost the 1868 election because the electorate did not reward him, but instead looked forward to new reforms. Disraeli was therefore forced to find ways to appeal to a new electorate. He did this by promising new reforms of his own, and a new brand of Conservatism.

New ideas for the Conservatives
The 1867 Reform Act and the reorganisation of the Conservative Party at grass roots by J.A. Gorst was subsequently labelled 'Tory democracy'. This title was used by Randolph Churchill in the 1880s in an attempt to rekindle the reforming zeal he felt existed in the 1870s. Disraeli himself used the expression 'One-nation Conservatism' to describe the ethos behind his reforms. Instead of supporting only the narrow interests of the aristocracy, Disraeli believed that serving the interests of working men was the only way to safeguard British institutions at all. Disraeli's ideas are revealed in the novels he wrote as a young man. In *Sybil* (1845) he explored the relationship between aristocrats and the rural poor. He wrote simply that: 'the Palace is unsafe if the cottage isn't happy'. One-nation Conservatism may simply have been a somewhat romantic idea that the classes could be united, but he had a pragmatic way of trying to achieve this. He attacked the Liberals as 'Little Englanders' because of their timid foreign policy. He argued that the Liberal attack on privilege really only favoured the middle classes and this was 'anti-national' and 'odious to the English people'. Finally he advocated the strengthening of the British Empire as a means to secure Britain's Great Power status in the future. He identified the Conservatives as the party of patriotism.

Disraeli's reforms were far-reaching

The Conservatives won the election of 1874 and returned 350 seats, as opposed to the Liberals' 245 and 57 for the Irish Home Rulers. Nevertheless, Disraeli was already an old man and lacked some of the energy of his youth. He greeted news of the victory with a sigh: 'Ah, power, it has come too late'. Although this was his second ministry (the first lasted a few months in 1868), Disraeli described becoming Prime Minister as like 'reaching the top of the greasy pole'. Some of the Conservative reforms appear to have been a response to Liberal reforms in the previous period, and Disraeli was reliant on the work of Richard Cross for his domestic reforms.

The reforms of Disraeli

► The Public Health Act 1875 laid down what the responsibilities of local authorities were and therefore greatly improved the Liberal legislation of 1872 which had been complex and hindered by a reluctance to spend money on it. A range of measures were identified, from burials to contaminated food.

► The Artisans Dwelling Act 1875 gave local authorities the power to purchase and demolish unhealthy slums. Landlords objected to the legislation being compulsory, but Joseph Chamberlain took up the opportunity as Mayor of Birmingham to replace poor housing there. This act was a fulfilment of Disraeli's promise to the electorate in 1872. He had argued that the Conservatives would promote a policy of 'air and light'. He stated that 'the health of the people is the most important question for a statesman'.

► The Sale of Food and Drugs Act 1875 prevented the 'adulteration' of food or drink and banned the malpractice of salting or watering down beer.

► The Enclosures Act 1876 preserved common land against private ownership and was the origin of the notion of green belts.

► Environmental legislation was passed under the Rivers Act (1876) which made it illegal to dump anything in rivers and so preserved rivers from poisonous liquids.

► Factory Acts (1874 and 1878) limited working hours.

► The Conspiracy and Protection of Property Act 1875 legalised peaceful picketing and thus overturned the Liberal act of 1871. This was a popular measure with trade unions. Alexander MacDonald, an engineering union leader, remarked that: 'the Conservatives have done more for the working class in five years, than the Liberals have done in fifty'. Disraeli was convinced this legislation would win the 'lasting affection' of the working classes.

- The Employers and Workmen Act 1876 abolished the idea that a breach of contract by a worker was a criminal offence. Instead, both employees and, for the first time, employers would be liable as a civil offence.

- Sandon's Education Act 1876 set up bodies to make sure that children attended school and gave them powers to assist parents to fund school attendance, although this was not compulsory.

- Merchant Shipping Act 1876. Another 'permissive' (not compulsory) piece of legislation. Shipowners were able to put seamen's lives at risk by overloading or failing to repair ships, secure in the knowledge they could claim compensation if they sank. Samuel Plimsoll forced Disraeli to legislate for a loading line on every ship, but there was little regulation about where the line was drawn.

Disraeli has been accused of insincerity
Disraeli came from a middle-class background, but he was ambitious. He was eager to lead the party but got his chance quite late in life which may explain the burst of reforms in the second ministry. Although he was ennobled by Queen Victoria, he died in 1881 shortly after his election defeat. Criticisms of Disraeli usually stem less from this ambition to be in power, but more from the apparent insincerity of his ideas. The existence of 'one-nation Conservativism' in his early novels does suggest that he had long-held views, but there was certainly mileage in winning over the new electorate too. This may have been the greater achievement; he was able to help his party through a critical transition phase and laid the foundations of a popular Conservative Party.

Disraeli achieved a great deal but some of his reforms lacked the compulsory element
Disraeli completely ignored the Irish Home Rulers and the Land League, despite the mounting land problems in Ireland. He felt that the Irish were as troublesome as the Balkans and had little time for these nationalist movements. His reforms retained the expediency which had been evident in the 1867 Reform Act in that they were designed to win over voters. However, it should also be noted that it was usually opposition from within the Conservative Party that reduced the compulsory nature of the social reforms.

Disraeli was defeated in 1880
By 1880, Britain had been involved in two unpopular imperial wars which Gladstone condemned very effectively in the so-called Midlothian Campaign. However, after 1876 there was a lack of social reform caused by Disraeli's interest in foreign affairs, but also by the obstruction tactics of 59 Irish MPs. These men, eager to get reform for Ireland, would use up parliamentary time by filibustering (talking just to waste time). They hoped to get the government's attention in this way, but failed. Conservative Party organisation at grass roots was inferior to the Liberals, costing them votes. Perhaps the biggest factor in the Conservative defeat

was the rise of unemployment at the beginning of the so-called Great Depression. Although this represented only a slowing down in Britain's growth, there was widespread concern about foreign competition. In agriculture, poor harvests and the importation of American grain caused widespread bankruptcy for farmers and unemployment amongst labourers. The second ministry nevertheless achieved a great deal, especially in health and sanitation, trade union rights and slum clearance. Again, like the 1867 Reform Act, Disraeli successfully steered between the ultras and the more liberal views of his party. He was a theatrical character who added colour to British political life and he was flamboyant and popular with the monarch. Lytton Strachey once wrote that Disraeli's second ministry was: 'six years of enchantment, of excitement... of glory, of romance'.

Foreign policy

The aim of British foreign policy in the second half of the nineteenth century was to preserve British interests and to protect the United Kingdom. The greatest threat to Britain was from other European powers, and, to a much lesser extent, from the USA. From 1815, the European nations had subscribed to the preservation of a balance of power. In the 1820s, attempts had been made to preserve Europe's frontiers and to act in concert to resolve any disputes. Although this had failed, there was an equilibrium between the leading states of Europe. However, in the 1860s, this balance was altered, not by France as before, but by the emergence of a united Italy and a united Germany. These new states were eager to assert themselves as great powers. Nevertheless, Britain continued to believe that its interests could be best served if no one power dominated the continent as Napoleonic France had done. It aimed to influence other European powers, not through alliances, but by diplomacy. Only in Belgium did Britain have a commitment to preserve another country's integrity, following an agreement in 1839.

France had been Britain's main rival until the 1850s
British policy for the first half of the century was concerned with the containment of France. However, the rise to power of Napoleon III led to closer relations between France and Britain. Free trade agreements, such as the Cobden-Chevalier Treaty of 1860, confirmed this. It wasn't until the 1880s, when the two countries became involved in imperial expansion in Africa and Asia, that relations took a severe turn for the worst. Nevertheless, in 1875, Disraeli dramatically secured shares in the Suez Canal in order to prevent French hegemony in the Eastern Mediterranean. The sell-off of this important waterway was prompted by the bankruptcy of the Khedive of Egypt, but Disraeli was aware of the strategic importance of Suez. By denying the French shares in the canal, it would prevent their dominance of Egypt too. The value of Britain's shares grew to £24 million in 1898 and by negotiating a reduction in canal tolls, costs of shipping goods to India, South East Asia and the Pacific fell by 75%.

Anglo-Russian relations were poor

Britain feared Russia's geo-strategic position which put her close to British India, and later, British possessions in China. Britain was also aware of the size of Russia's continental land forces. Britain saw Russia as particularly dangerous when in combination with the central European autocracies of Germany and Austria-Hungary. These three Empires formed the *Dreikaiserbund* in 1872, an agreement which turned into a military alliance in 1881. Both Russia and Britain feared the ambitions of the other, particularly in the Near East.

The Eastern question: uncertainty about the future of the Near East

Apparently about to collapse at any moment, the decaying Ottoman Empire forced the European powers to consider what might replace it. The likely outcome was Russian hegemony in the Balkans and Turkey, with small and weak states making up the bulk of the rest of the territory. British policy in the mid-nineteenth century was to try to preserve the Ottoman Empire because of the possibility that a dominant Russia might be able to sever Britain's trade arteries (with India and the Far East) in the eastern Mediterranean. The notion that there was a Russian threat can be challenged. It could be argued that Russia's designs to control the Straits at Constantinople were motivated less by a desire for conquest than by a desire for secure frontiers, or a buffer zone, a practice with which the British were all too familiar in India. John Gleason (*The Genesis of Russophobia in Great Britain*, 1972) has argued convincingly for such a case, while Paul Kennedy (*The Realities Behind Diplomacy*,1985) has explained that the contemporary British press created the image of an insatiable, grasping Russian Empire.

The Crimean War (1854–56) resulted from 'Russophobia'

British views of Russian intentions in the Near East were coloured by unguarded remarks the Tsar had made during an official visit in 1844 in which he had suggested the partition of Turkish lands. The spread of Russian influence in the Middle East and central Asia seemed to indicate a plan of expansion. Many felt that the ultimate result of this policy would be the invasion of India, or, in the very least, the fomenting of rebellion amongst the tribes and peoples under British rule. Russell, the Whig leader told Lord Aberdeen that 'the question must be settled by war, and if we do not stop the Russians on the Danube we shall have to stop them on the Indus'. The Russians viewed their regime as benign and paternal. The English regarded the Russian government as the worst kind of autocracy; cruel where it was not inefficient. War broke out when the Turks were threatened by a Russian occupation of the mouth of the Danube, and their fleet was destroyed at Sinope, but there was a background of 'Russophobia' which made the public clamour for war in Britain irresistible.

The defeat of Russia in 1856 was temporary

Russia went over to the offensive again in the 1860s. The government felt strong enough to conduct difficult operations in the Caucasus to subjugate the peoples there. By the late 1860s they had forcibly depopulated the areas of greatest resistance and crossed the mountain ranges to abut the Ottoman Empire again. In 1870 St Petersburg renounced the neutralisation clause of the Treaty of Paris, taking advantage of French and Prussian distraction in the war of 1870–71. At the London Conference in 1871, Gladstone agreed to the abandonment of the terms of the Treaty of Paris.

Turkish atrocities shocked the British people

The Treaty of Paris proved to be an interlude rather than a lasting settlement in the Balkans too. A rebellion in 1875 in Bosnia and Herzogovina testified to the continuing antagonism of Christians and Muslims in the region. In particular it proved that the Russian motive for intervention, ostensibly to protect Christians throughout the Balkans, was still valid. Consequently Disraeli did not sign the Berlin Memorandum – a demand from the Great Powers to the Ottoman Empire insisting on fair treatment of Christians. In a short time the rebellion spread to Serbia, Montenegro and Bulgaria, but the Turks proved that their empire was maintained adequately by military force. Atrocities, which seem to be so tragically characteristic of warfare in the Balkans, were committed on a large scale. The infamous Bashi Bazouks, irregular troops of the Ottoman army, butchered 12,000 Bulgarian civilians. However, Disraeli clung to his faith in a strong Turkey as a bulwark to Russian aggression. The sacrifice of Balkan rebels was justified, he reasoned, if the Straits remained beyond the grasp of the Tsar.

The Liberals were critical of the Conservatives' 'unethical' foreign policy

Beaconsfield's policy came in for sharp criticism from his rival Gladstone, but many Liberals felt Gladstone went too far in his publication of 'The Bulgarian Horrors' which was tantamount to a public declaration that the Russians should intervene in the Balkans. With dismay, the public soon learned that the Russians had done exactly that in November 1876. After direct negotiations, Russia gave Britain assurances that neither the Straits nor Constantinople were to be invested. Disraeli obtained further assurances that the Russians were not interested in the Suez Canal or India and reciprocated with a promise of neutrality in any Russian conflict. The Russian declaration of war that followed in April 1877 was thus made with the apparent acceptance of the British. In fact, this was due less to Conservative 'approval' of Russian actions and more to do with the divided nature of British public opinion. The government simply could not oppose the Russians because most of the British people sympathised with the oppressed Christians and not the Turks.

Turkish resistance to Russia won back British sympathy

The resistance of the Turks won the public back to a more traditional anti-Russian stance. The defence of Plevna from June to December 1877 became a symbol of Turkish courage against great odds. However, when Plevna fell, Turkish resistance weakened and, by January 1878, the Russians were making rapid progress towards Constantinople. With the fall of Adrianople, only 100 miles from the capital, Disraeli felt he could not trust the Russians to halt and ordered a fleet to the Bosphorous. Crowds in Britain signalled their approval and Gladstone was jeered, having his windows smashed by patriotic mobs. As the Royal Navy raced to the Straits, the Russian troops reached the outskirts of Constantinople known as San Stefano. While the Turks prepared to defend their city and Disraeli gathered an expeditionary force, the prospect of a war between Russia and Britain seemed likely.

Russia concluded San Stefano: a treaty to preserve its interests
The Russian forces were in no shape to continue the war, let alone take on Britain. The dash to Constantinople left them exhausted and supply routes stretched to the limit. The likelihood of a second Plevna was deemed beyond them. In addition a counter-attack by the remaining Turkish troops was a distinct possibility. Consequently the decision to make a quick settlement before the British became involved is easy to understand. The Treaty of San Stefano of March 1878 was opposed bitterly by Britain and Austria. The terms completely ignored the arrangements made prior to the war. Under the Treaty of San Stefano, Serbia, Montenegro and Romania were to be fully independent. Bessarabia was to be ceded to Russia giving her direct access to the banks of the Danube, and putting her back in the position she occupied in 1853. Most shocking however was the concept of a 'Big Bulgaria', a Balkan superstate that would stretch across the region from the Black Sea to the Aegean. The clause which declared that Russian officers would initially supervise this new state was tantamount to Russian control of the Balkans as a whole, and, worse still, gave the Russians access to the Mediterranean. The Straits and Constantinople would no longer interest the Tsar, there would be a sympathetic power dominating the Aegean.

There was a jingoistic reaction against Russia
Disraeli's calling up of the Reserves marked a determination to fight over this issue. Music halls resounded with a song which ran: 'We don't want to fight, but, by Jingo, if we do, we've got the ships, we've got the men and we've got the money too'. The term 'jingoism' entered the English language to refer to a vulgar form of patriotism. The Liberal radicals were critical of the Tories' belligerence, while the movement of Indian troops to Malta was criticised in India since they felt that, in the event of a war with Russia, the troops would be needed on the Indo-Afghan border. Generally, however, the idea of a war with Russia was popular. Certainly the threat of war was taken seriously in St Petersburg. In Russian central Asia an invasion force for India was prepared, and a diplomatic mission was despatched to Afghanistan to pave the way to the Indus.

The Congress of Berlin (June–July 1878) averted war
The Congress of Berlin showed that while determined to contemplate war if they obtained no satisfaction, both sides favoured negotiation above all else. Disraeli

and Salisbury (the Foreign Secretary) certainly achieved all they set out to do; it was only later, when the Balkans was convulsed by another rebellion in 1885, that Salisbury complained he and his Prime Minister had 'backed the wrong horse at Berlin'. In the short term British success was not in doubt. Russian armies had been checked and removed from the Balkans, the 'Big Bulgaria' project was dropped, a serious war had been averted, the island of Cyprus (ceded by Turkey) was to act as a landing stage for the relief of Constantinople should it find itself besieged in the future, and the Turks reiterated assurances of fair treatment of Christian subjects. Most important of all was the fact that soured relations between Austria, Russia and Germany led to the break up of the *Dreikaiserbund*, the military alliance which posed a major threat to Britain. Salisbury later considered this to be the greatest achievement of the settlement.

The Empire

Disraeli was an advocate of imperialism
In 1872, at Crystal Palace, Disraeli had warned that unless Britain developed the Empire as a strong economic and political entity under the crown, it would be eclipsed by the great continental powers of America, Russia and Germany. The speech may have been intended for domestic consumption, to prove that the Conservatives were the party of patriotism, but those in the imperial possessions of India and the Cape (Southern Africa) sensed that this meant Britain must make the Empire secure. Nevertheless, Disraeli was disapproving when his subordinates, Lord Lytton and Sir Bartle Frere, took action. This suggests that Disraeli was not prepared to take on additional colonies. In the 1840s he had described them as 'millstones around our necks' and many British governments appeared to be just as reluctant.

Russian threats prompted the British invasion of Afghanistan
When news of a Russian mission to Kabul reached London after the Congress of Berlin, Disraeli favoured negotiation first, but he soon lost control of his proconsul, Lord Lytton. Lytton was convinced that Russia wanted to absorb all of Central Asia and threaten the frontiers of India. The solution to this problem was easy to reach. Some favoured the defence of India from within her own frontiers, avoiding the expense of occupation of new lands, avoiding the antagonism of the tribesmen inside and on the fringes of Afghanistan, and avoiding the repeat of the costly First Afghan War (1838–42). Others, including Lytton, wanted a firm 'forward' approach. This might involve either the occupation of Afghanistan, or it might simply mean alliance with Afghanistan and the ability to fight Russia in the hills of that country. Lytton was exasperated by the attitude of the Afghan Amir, Sher Ali, believing his hostility stemmed from the fact that he was already relying on Russian support. The belief was misguided. When Lytton ordered troops into Afghanistan to establish a rival British mission, the Russians abandoned the Amir.

The Tsar simply could not risk a conflict with Britain so soon after the bitter humiliation and isolation caused by the Congress of Berlin.

The Second Afghan War 1878–80 ended without a permanent occupation
The British invasion of 1878–79 was successful but the Resident (diplomat) who was installed was murdered as soon as British troops were withdrawn. An avenging army forced their way to the capital a second time and the Amir abdicated. The vacant throne was filled by Abdur Rahman, a man determined to maintain the independence of his country. Abdur Rahman faced rebellion as soon as he took power, and a British force was overwhelmed at Maiwand and besieged. Lord Roberts marched through the wilderness to relieve the garrison and defeat the Afghan rebels at Kandahar. The British withdrew their forces once they had secured the co-operation of the new ruler. The war convinced the Russians that Britain was determined to prevent any power from influencing Afghanistan.

Southern Africa was to be confederated under British rule
The Colonial Secretary, Lord Canarvon, aimed to form a confederation of southern Africa as he had done with Canada in 1867. He established, through Sir Theophilus Shepstone, that the Afrikaner states of Transvaal and Orange Free State were generally hostile to incorporation but they were eager for British support against the Zulu kingdom. Zulus and Boers (the name given to Afrikaner farmers) had clashed since the formation of the republics in the 1830s; settlers knew that the Zulus were a formidable nation whose social organisation was based on military lines. Burgers, the president of the Transvaal, agreed to surrender his state's independence in 1877 because of bankruptcy. In return he received assurances that independence would be restored once the Zulu threat had been neutralised. When Bartle Frere became High Commissioner of South Africa, he was determined to press forward with confederation. He ordered the destruction of the Zulu kingdom and aimed to annex the Boer states permanently.

The Zulu War 1878–79 altered the balance of power in southern Africa
The British invasion of Zululand suffered an early setback when a British force of 1,600 was surprised and overwhelmed by 20,000 Zulus at Isandhlwana (1879). A small detachment at Rorke's Drift nevertheless held off a Zulu attack and prevented the Zulus invading Natal. Disraeli was angry that the unilateral action of Frere had led to war and he faced much criticism. The public mood was little improved by the embarrassing death of the Prince Imperial, a member of the French royal family who was attached to the British army. Nevertheless, the Zulus were defeated at Ulundi in July 1879 and Ceteweyo, the king, was sent into exile. The defeat of the Zulus led to Boer demands for their independence, and they rose in rebellion in 1881. Whilst Gladstone's government was negotiating, the Boers attacked a British force at Majuba Hill and routed it. There was an expectation that the Liberals would sent a punitive expedition to avenge this defeat, but Gladstone refused. The issue of confederation therefore remained unresolved.

Historical controversies

P.R. Ghosh in *Style and Substance in Disraelian Social Reform* (1987) argued that the Disraeli's second ministry marked a genuine willingness by Conservatives to embrace social reform. He also believed the reforms to be of great significance. Bruce Coleman, in *Conservativism and the Conservative Party in Nineteenth Century Britain* (1988) disagreed. He pointed out that Disraeli offered nothing new to the Party. It was traditionalist and its emphasis was on continuity. John Walton concurred, pointing out that Disraeli's presentation was more remarkable than his policies. John Vincent also highlighted the idea that some changes were taking place inside the Conservative Party that had little do with Disraeli. It was changing from the Party of the squires to the Party of business, the suburbs and the 'genteel south-east'. Martin Pugh demonstrated it was the way that Conservative support grew in the English boroughs and generally held on in the counties, that preserved the Party from extinction. E.J. Feuchtwanger (*Democracy and Empire*, 1985) argued that Disraeli believed the role of the party was not to harass the country. In other words, he saw his role as the opposite of the Liberals who seemed intent on change. Professor Paul Smith felt that the reforms were limited and made little impact on the 'established institutions'. Overseas, S.R Stembridge and F. Harcourt argued that Disraeli was quite consistent in his views on the British Empire. Disraeli saw the Empire as a resource for the British army, but opposed expansion and was concerned by the burden of maintaining the sprawling colonial inheritance. A similar disagreement has arisen over Gladstone. T. A. Jenkins argued that Gladstone was the major factor in holding the Liberals together, but also the cause of the Party split later in 1886. Richard Shannon felt that Gladstone's return to politics in 1875, after a semi-retirement to study more theology, ruined the Party's radicalism, and E.J. Feuchtwanger felt he stayed too long, although his ideas had 'perennial validity'. Christopher Harvie and H.C.G Matthew also took a positive view of Gladstone's reforms, declaring that the propertied and labouring classes had 'collaborated in a great clearing of the decks of the liberal ship of state'.

Tutorial

Progress questions
1. What improvements were made for the working classes in the period 1867–80?

2. Was Disraeli 'unprincipled?'

3. Was Disraeli an imperialist?

4. Account for the defeat of the Liberals in 1874 and the Conservatives in 1880.

5. How successful was British foreign policy between 1868 and 1880?

Seminar discussion

Prepare a debate, with supporting evidence, to argue that Disraeli was little more than an opportunist. Then prepare an argument, again supported by examples, to show that Gladstone was a failure. Can you argue the opposite sides to these approaches?

Practical assignment

1. Try to summarise this chapter in six paragraphs, dealing with the most important points in each section. Keep a list of the views of historians, so that you can use them in essays and assignments.

2. Use these notes to help you answer an essay question of no more than 1,500 words entitled: ' "*The greatest reforming ministry of the nineteenth century*". Does this statement apply more appropriately to Gladstone or Disraeli between 1867 and 1880?'

Study tips

1. It is important to know the *reforms* which Gladstone passed in this period and their significance (use a mnemonic to remember them – e.g. 'jet blac cupid'). Some of the reforms were a success, but many were not. It would be worthwhile reviewing a list of reforms to establish which worked and which failed. It is a good idea to establish what your criterion of success actually is. A useful idea is to ask 'what were his aims' and 'did he fulfil them with *this* piece of legislation'? This is a better tactic than trying to judge them by the standards of the twenty-first century; this would be an error known as relativism. We should not forget that he was a Victorian and you should become familiar with Victorian and liberal values.

2. Try to reach *conclusions* on how the reforms show us Gladstone's motives, the significance of the first steps towards state intervention, the application of Gladstone's principles, or how they show up Gladstone's inconsistencies.

3. Try to do the same with Disraeli's reforms. Bear in mind that Disraeli himself was often more concerned with foreign affairs and much of the groundwork was done by Richard Cross. This could be seen as good leadership, in that he was making the best use of his subordinates, or it could be seen as the behaviour of a charlatan.

4. Be aware that both Disraeli and Gladstone tried to uphold Britain's interests, but that both had different interpretations of how this was to be done.

3

Ireland, 1868-1914

One-minute summary – Ireland was part of the United Kingdom throughout the nineteenth century, but there were frequent calls for the establishment of Home Rule (self-government) with a parliament in Dublin. Alongside this political question was Ireland's economic condition. Although industry developed in the northern city of Belfast, much of southern and western Ireland remained agrarian and poor. Falling land values and low productivity led to the eviction of tenants from rented property. This, and memories of the hardships of the mid-century famine, acted as a spur to more violent resistance to British rule. Successive governments sought to find a solution to Ireland's problems. The Conservatives favoured economic reforms and firm government, whilst the Liberals under Gladstone sought first to tackle the evictions before turning to the idea of Home Rule for Ireland. This solution foundered on the rock of Ulster, the Protestant counties of the north who refused to accept minority status or the possibility of sectarian persecution.

In this chapter you will learn about:

▶ the Irish question and the legacy of Union
▶ Fenianism and Irish nationalism
▶ Parnell and the land war
▶ the Home Rule question
▶ the emergence of Ulster Unionism from 1885.

The Irish question and the legacy of Union

Ireland in the late 1700s

Agricultural boom years for the peasantry were caused by the Napoleonic Wars which stimulated demand for cloth, leather, food and fodder. Wheat was one of the most important crops after 1815 until the repeal of the Corn Laws in 1846. Potatoes and pigs tended to be grown for their own consumption. In 1800, the Union of England and Ireland was forged in order to safeguard Britain's security. During the Revolutionary wars, Ireland had been subject to rebellion and French invasion. There was concern that Ireland would be a springboard for an invasion of Britain.

1815-1846: years of hardship

As in England, the years after the wars were hard. The population had doubled and farming plots had been continually subdivided until they were uneconomical.

Crop failures followed because of wet summers and poor harvests. Reliance on potatoes meant that malnutrition was prevalent (again, this was also a problem in England as William Cobbett noted in the 1830s in light of the Swing Riots). In 1838, Britain introduced poor relief (England in 1834), but this was too little to help. Part of the problem lay in rents. Landowners were eager to improve the land against these poor economic conditions. However, rents were sublet to tenants who also sublet and each, in turn, tried to create a profit. Evictions followed if rents could not be paid. Evictions, like rents, could be arbitrary and without notice. In England, economic forces were also driving the poorest labourers and peasants from the land. In Ulster, there was a joint interest between tenant and owner. The tenant had to be compensated and could sell that 'interest' and he could sue for the improvements he had made. Emigration increased, but not solely to the USA as is commonly believed because the Irish poor could not afford the passage. Most emigrated to England and Scotland, particularly London, Liverpool and Glasgow.

The worst famine years were 1845–46
In 1845, wheat and potatoes failed in England and Ireland. Peel sent Indian corn and private owners also sent help. Peel then repealed the Corn Laws which, in the longer term, released corn from the USA into Ireland and England. This did end the famine, but ruined agriculture. Ulster, which had a large linen industry, was relatively unaffected. It continued to develop along industrial lines. In 1846, the potatoes failed again, but now there were no incomes to stave off famine and disaster struck. Property sales increased dramatically (one in six properties changed hands). New owners demanded better returns for their purchases and decided to enlarge holdings into more economically viable units. This resulted in more evictions. The government insisted that 48 hours' notice be given to let the Poor Law authorities prepare themselves.

The legacy of the famine was political opposition
Irish Americans remembered the hardship and the Atlantic crossings with bitterness. The Irish population fell from 8 million to 5.5 million through death or emigration. Recently, Irish historians have regarded this famine as the fault of the British and little more than a genocide. A genocide is a deliberate policy and there is no evidence at all that the British government wanted to see the extermination of the Irish. Irishmen were viewed as second-class citizens by many in England, but Peel's actions to save the people from starvation contradict the genocide argument. Nor was the neglect of Irish people entirely the fault of the English. The roads of Ireland were often small and unmetalled, turning into quagmires after rains, and stricken areas were remote and difficult to reach. Trying to get supplies to those in most need was difficult. There were conflicting interests too, as English rural poor faced hardship at the same time. In Ireland, corrupt local officials sold food to the highest bidder. As always, it was not starvation that killed the

majority, but malnutrition, and this affected millions of Englishmen and Irishmen before the crisis years of 1845–47, and after.

Falling land values led to a new round of evictions later

In 1868, Gladstone came to power and passed the Land Act of Tenancy (Ulster's procedure transferred to the southern Irish). However, tenants were forced to leave the land because of 'rack-renting', the practice where rents were ratcheted up in order to get tenants out. This happened because landlords themselves were facing bankruptcy.

Political reforms were demanded from the 1820s onwards

Daniel O'Connell demanded political freedom for Irish Catholics and the Repeal of the Act of Union (with England). In 1828, the British government passed the Catholic Emancipation Act following the lobbying of the Catholic Association. All positions of government were opened to Catholics, except the very highest (such as the monarchy). However, O'Connell's oratory and agitation had won little sympathy in England. Lord Melbourne and Sir Robert Peel prevented O'Connell's demand for a repeal of union from being successful by the abolition of tithes, the establishment of the Poor Law, the creation of the Royal Irish Constabulary, the suppression of secret societies, the foundation of the national school board (assisting the poor with some education), the construction of Queen's University Belfast and the offer of grants for the training of Catholic priests (such as the Maynooth Grant). O'Connell was also opposed by Ulster Protestants, and he had persistent critics in Young Ireland (a secular, rather than Catholic organisation that was attracted to the notion of revolution, though only as a last resort). Sections of the Irish people who feared one demagogic leader were also doubtful, and his movement was weakened by the social divisions of class (the middle class were against the greater expense of reforms). O'Connell's agitation therefore petered out without success.

Fenianism and Irish nationalism

The Fenians believed Ireland's only solution was liberation through violence

This group was founded in 1857 in Chicago, USA. It recommended the murder of landlords, condemned the Catholic church and called for a general uprising, which was ignored in Ireland. They carried out 'outrages' including murders and bombings, such as the murder of a policeman in Manchester in 1867 and the detonation of a bomb at Clerkenwell in London which injured 400 people. The Fenians also attempted to invade Canada, but their attacks were a farce.

Pacification was Gladstone's mission

Gladstone aimed to 'pacify Ireland' and passed the Disestablishment of the Church of Ireland Act (1869), and the Land Act (1870). The Irish interpreted this as the British giving way in the face of violence. Irish nationalism developed throughout the period as it had a wide appeal. Republicans tended to speak only in terms of Home Rule, or self-government, rather than independence. However, many emigrants to Australia or America took with them their ambivalence towards British rule, or a desire to avoid politics altogether and start a new life. Fenians, and other secret societies, were prepared to suffer death or imprisonment for the liberation of Ireland. Faced with the might of the British army, and police, terrorist attacks were the only practical tactics that could be employed. Yet terrorists were to find there was a political cost to this approach, and the alienation of popular support undermined the concessions they might have wrung from the British government.

The Home Rule League and the land war

Protestant landowner Charles Parnell set up the Home Rule League having been a leading member of the Land League (Michael Davitt's movement for land reform set up in 1879). He aimed to obstruct the English parliament with filibustering (talking constantly to use up parliamentary time) and destruction of the land owners in Ireland using the Land League. Parnell hinted that direct action and violence were necessary. The Second Land Bill, to rectify the shortcomings of the first, was introduced in 1880, but did not get through until 1881 by which time a Coercion Bill was necessary to cope with an increase in violence in Ireland. Gladstone's Bill had offered what the Irish tenant wanted, namely 'the three Fs'; fixity of tenure, free sale and fair rents, but Parnell encouraged boycotting of the new measures. Forster, the Irish Secretary, imprisoned Parnell at Kilmainham for stirring up the escalating violence. Arson, murder and cattle maiming continued. In 1882 Gladstone released Parnell in the 'Kilmainham Treaty' to calm the violence in return for an Arrears Act (1883) which wiped out rents not paid during what became known as the 'land war'. However, the Chief Secretary of Ireland, Lord Cavendish, and his Permanent Under Secretary, T.E. Burke, both of whom were sympathetic to Irish grievances, were murdered on their arrival in Ireland in Phoenix Park, Dublin. Irishmen and Englishmen were shocked at the action, and its ferocity. The perpetrators were soon captured and hanged.

Parnell and the Conservatives

When the Liberals seemed to offer no more concessions after 1883, Parnell looked to the Conservatives. Lord Randolph Churchill was a radical, eager to resurrect the Conservatives' reforming image which he believed had been created by Disraeli. Churchill hinted at the concessions that could be made to Ireland, and, in June 1885, Gladstone's government was brought down when Conservatives and Irish MPs voted together. The new Ministry, led by Salisbury, ended the Coercion Act of 1881, passed a Land Reform Bill (Ashbourne's) which gave financial assistance to tenants to buy their own land. At the general election in

November 1885, the Conservative–Parnell coalition kept the Liberals out, but further Conservative reform, and especially Home Rule, seemed unlikely. Home Rule seemed to be a threat to the unity of the United Kingdom, and also to the survival of the British Empire. Some feared that Ireland would swiftly move towards independence and this would make her an ideal springboard for a foreign power to invade England. This had been Britain's fear when French troops landed in Ireland during a rebellion in 1798, and this itself had been the main motive behind the Act of Union which had brought Ireland into the United Kingdom in the first place. Parnell's argument was simply that Ireland was entitled to its own parliament in Dublin.

The Home Rule question

Gladstone moved Ireland towards Home Rule

Gladstone made moves towards Home Rule sometime before 1885 (probably as a result of seeing Norwegian self-government in action), but the return of 85 nationalist MPs from Ireland, following the new Franchise Act of 1884, persuaded him of the need for this move. Gladstone's son, Herbert, announced his father's conversion in a newspaper article. This may have been a deliberate ploy to test public opinion and has come to be known as 'flying the Hawarden kite' (Hawarden was Gladstone's home). The 1886 Bill was not popular. There was a strong current of opinion against it in Britain, although Gladstone lost in the Commons by a narrow margin: 343 voted against, 313 for it. Significantly, 93 Liberals had voted against the government. Gladstone then miscalculated. He thought that going to the country on the issue would have returned a greater Liberal majority, but he was unpopular in Britain after the death of Gordon (1885) and setbacks in South Africa (1881). The result was the defeat of the Liberals in a general election (where they dropped to 191 seats). Worst still, the Liberals were split. The majority of the 93 rebellious MPs called themselves Liberal-Unionists, and, in time, many of them transferred their allegiance permanently to the Conservatives.

Killing Home Rule by kindness

Between 1886 and 1906, the Conservatives aimed to kill Home Rule by granting reforms. However, the Conservative Irish Chief Secretary, Arthur Balfour, promised 'twenty years of strong government'. He stated: 'I shall be as relentless as Cromwell in enforcing obedience to the law, but, at the same time, I shall be as radical as any reformer in redressing grievances'. In 1886, William O'Brien and John Dillon organised the so-called 'plan of campaign' in which tenants only paid what they thought was a fair rent, and, if more was demanded they would refuse to pay anything, transferring the money to a fighting fund. Violence broke out again as evictions followed. In response, the government passed the Crimes Act (1887) which gave the police and magistrates wide powers of arrest and

---

The Liberal Government
Aim to introduce a degree of Home Rule in order to preserve the Union of Britain and Ireland. This would, it was thought, satisfy Nationalist demands.

Conservative and Unionist Party
Home Rule for the Irish would lead to demands for Home Rule across the British Empire, it was feared. Conservative-Unionists wanted to strengthen the bonds of Empire with all the 'White Dominions'. In addition, a Dublin parliament would deal unfairly, it was feared, with the Protestant minority of Ireland in Ulster and around Dublin.

Irish Nationalists
The moderates wanted to gain Home Rule and reap the rewards with the Irish people in terms of popularity and therefore exclusive political power. The extremists (Republicans) after 1906 felt that Home Rule was not enough and complete independence was needed. They were prepared to use violence to force the British government to make the concessions they wanted. Their rise coincided with a Gaelic revival and disillusionment with the lack of progress by the moderates.

Ulster Unionists
The Protestant, industrialised and urbanised north had little sympathy with Catholic, agrarian southerners. They aimed to preserve the Union at all costs and were prepared to fight.

Fig. 3. Ireland: aims and methods.

imprisonment. It was renewed annually until 1890. However, the Conservatives also made a positive contribution to Ireland by avoiding the confrontations associated with political reform.

Conservative reforms brought peace to Ireland
In 1903 a royal visit was a great success and seemed to indicate that Irishmen would remain loyal to the King-Emperor. Economic measures also brought Ireland peace. The 1891 Land Purchase Act extended Ashborne's legislation. Wyndham's 1903 Land Act loaned peasants money to buy their own land at low rates of interest. Congested District Boards (1891) assisted those in over-populated areas of the south and west. A light railway was built. Fishermen were brought in from Scotland to train the Irish, boats and better nets were handed over to them. Lace making was subsidised. Balfour organised a relief campaign when potato blight reappeared in western Ireland. Land drainage, fencing and the introduction of modern farming methods were also effective. The Irish viewed Gladstone's concession as evidence that the British gave way when forced or threatened. The economic measures of the late nineties brought a lull in the unrest. For the English, there was a simple aim: to see a contented Ireland without violence.

Parnell fell from favour over adultery
Parnell was at the height of his popularity in 1890 after letters published in *The Times*, which alleged his involvement in the Phoenix Park murders, were found to be a forgery. An enquiry discovered that the forger was an Irish journalist called

Piggott, but he fled arrest and committed suicide. Parnell was given a standing ovation in the Commons and there was a wave of sympathy for the cause of Irish Home Rule. He was nick-named the 'Uncrowned King of Ireland'. However, unknown to the public, Parnell was having an affair with a married woman. Katherine O'Shea spent nine years with Parnell and her husband tolerated it, knowing that he would get a share of his wife's aunt's will in return for keeping quiet. However, when the aunt died and the will was presented in 1889, O'Shea was dissatisfied and filed for divorce on grounds that his wife was an adulteress. In November 1890, the divorce went through, and Parnell was named. In the moral climate of the 1890s, this public revelation was scandalous. The expectation was that he should resign but Parnell insisted that he should remain. The Liberal Nonconformists shunned him, as did many Roman Catholic Irish MPs (44 out of the 70). Yet he refused to resign, arrogantly clinging to power. His health failed under the strain and he died in October 1891, aged only 45.

The impact of the Parnell scandal was catastrophic for the Home Rule cause
The Nationalists were bitterly divided. They directed more effort against each other than against the British government for several years. The whole momentum for Irish Home Rule faltered. F.S. Lyons described Parnell as someone who had wanted Irish Home Rule by what he considered the most efficient means: the use of parliament. Lyons rejected the idea that Parnell favoured force. Certainly there is evidence that, despite his fiery oratory, Parnell was as nervous as the government about the consequences of violent protest.

The Second Home Rule Bill was defeated in the Lords
The Second Home Rule Bill was introduced in 1893 when Gladstone, with the support of the 81 Irish Nationalist MPs, managed to defeat the combined Conservative-Unionist (as they now styled themselves) and Liberal-Unionist coalition. Gladstone piloted the Bill through the Commons himself, a performance Philip Magnus described as 'at the age of 83, [it] must be ranked among the supreme achievements of his life'. Yet it was in vain, the Bill was rejected by the Lords as 'unconstitutional', by 419 votes to 41. Gladstone wanted to fight an election so as to return with a mandate from the people to reduce the powers of the Lords, but his Cabinet colleagues refused and he resigned in 1894. He died four years later.

Ulster and Unionism

Nationalists and Unionists
However, in 1906 the Liberal victory in Britain meant that Home Rule demands would soon resurface. The Irish Nationalist movement, Sinn Fein, formed in the same year aimed for full independence. Arthur Griffith wanted the constitution of 1792 which gave Ireland its own parliament, but there was soon agreement that

this would be only the first step towards a complete break with Britain and the declaration of a republic. Ulstermen, Protestants from the counties of Antrim, Derry, Armagh and Down, and from Dublin, had no wish to be incorporated into a united Ireland under Catholic rule. They had aligned themselves with the Conservatives in 1886 when Randolph Churchill had remarked that Home Rule would mean 'Rome Rule'. The north had other differences too. Belfast was dominated by industry, particularly shipbuilding, whilst the rest of Ireland was mainly agricultural. Culturally, Ulstermen thought of themselves as more akin to the British than the Irish. They were distinct in custom, tradition, dialect, music, religion and sports. When there seemed to be the prospect of a new Home Rule bill from a parliament dominated by the Liberals in 1912, Edward Carson encouraged Ulstermen to sign a Covenant to resist it.

Conclusions – Gladstone attempted to change Ireland but failed

Gladstone made a particularly important effort for Ireland. It was not the number of reforms he passed, nor their failure, but the opposition he faced which is of particular significance. For most of the period Gladstone was in office, the situation in Ireland was appalling. A spate of assassinations, cattle maiming, rick burning, extortionate rents, evictions by high-handed local bailiffs, and obstructionist tactics in parliament by Irish MPs, demanded attention. However, some of the problems Gladstone was trying to solve were of his own making. His Second Irish Land Bill (introduced in 1880) was designed to rectify the problems partly created by his first Land Act of 1870 since it proposed compensation for evicted tenants. The Bill was piloted though the Commons by Gladstone personally in 58 sessions, but it was defeated by the Lords. Note that this blocking by the Lords was to be repeated with the Second Home Rule Bill in 1893. The upsurge of violence and boycotting forced Gladstone to accept the introduction of the Coercion Act (1881) even though he once vowed: 'Coercion – I hate the thing'. Yet he was able to deliver a Second Irish Land Act (granting compensation and the 3 Fs) in 1881, after the Coercion Act had been passed. These events indicate Gladstone's determination and courage; the strength of the opposition; that Irishmen felt violence had forced the Liberals to make more concessions; and that Liberalism was ill-suited to face the crisis of extremism or war (in this case a 'land war').

Gladstone and Parnell aimed to be the agents of peaceful change

Gladstone represented the best chance of bringing Home Rule to Ireland peacefully. Following the 'Kilmainham Treaty', he was able to reach a compromise with the Arrears Act in 1883, which was promised in return to a cessation of violence by the Irish Home Rule Movement. Parnell also wanted to use the parliamentary system, rather than direct action, to bring about change. However, too many of Parnell's supporters were prepared to use violence. The spectre of terrorism merely hardened the resolve of the British to oppose self-government.

Professor Dicey, author of the *England's Case against Home Rule* (1885) pointed out that Ireland needed to remain part of the Union if it was to develop. He argued that Home Rule would not solve Ireland's fundamental problems, namely, a weak agrarian economy. The opposition of the Commons MPs and the House of Lords defeated the progress towards Home Rule. Yet Gladstone and Parnell failed to take account of the Ulstermen too.

The failure of compromise was Ireland's greatest tragedy

The Conservative measures of the period 1890–1905 went a long way to solving some of Ireland's economic difficulties, but there was still unease with the continuation of English rule. Despite the split of the Irish Nationalists after Parnell's affair, Ireland continued to return Nationalist MPs in large numbers. At Mitchelstown, police shot three demonstrators and Balfour's dismissal of the incident earned him the title 'Bloody Balfour'. The establishment of Sinn Fein also indicates that a minority at least had moved beyond Home Rule. Even before the introduction of the Third Home Rule Bill, Ulstermen had pledged themselves to resist Irish independence.

Tutorial

Progress questions

1. Why did Irish Fenians and nationalists consider violence the solution to British rule between 1868 and 1900?

2. What measures did Gladstone introduce to pacify Ireland?

3. How did Parnell promote, but ultimately damage, the progress towards Irish Home Rule?

4. What were the arguments against Home Rule between 1886 and 1914?

Seminar discussion

1. How significant was Parnell in the progress towards Home Rule compared with other factors?

2. Read the extract below.

> Charles Stuart Parnell, 21 January 1885.
> 'We shall never gain anything from England unless we tread on her toes; we will never gain a sixpennyworth from her by conciliation. . . In 1880, I pledged myself that I should form one of an independent Irish Party to act in opposition to every English government.'

Which was the greatest obstacle to Ireland development: British intransigence or Irish extremism?

Practical assignment

1. Draw up a list of the Irish grievances and the attempts to solve them.

2. Compare the arguments for and against Home Rule. What benefits and burdens could it have brought to Ireland?

Study tips

1. It is worth noting that many of the grievances in Irish agriculture were similar to those in Britain, but there were added complications such as the sectarian divide.

2. Keep a list of arguments for and against Irish Home Rule. Note how progress towards Home Rule was obstructed by violence, which itself was caused by the hardships in Irish agriculture. A sense of martyrdom and struggle came to characterise the more extreme nationalist organisations but this, in turn, made the Ulster Protestants even more fearful of the consequences of rule by Dublin.

3. Note the connection between economic factors and political aspirations.

4

The Decline of Old Certainties, 1880–1898

One-minute summary – The relative decline of British industry and the country's diplomatic isolation signalled the end of the country's mid-century confidence. British farming was severely damaged by foreign competition, and, despite his parliamentary bills, Gladstone seemed unable to fulfil his ambitions for domestic reforms. His desire to pacify Ireland faltered because of opposition on both sides of the Irish Sea. He was drawn into a war in Egypt and he alienated the most talented man in his party – Joseph Chamberlain. Chamberlain was both a radical and an imperialist, who split the Liberals in 1886 and eventually joined the Conservatives. Salisbury, by contrast, skilfully contained the radical element of his party and won over the Liberal-Unionists, including Chamberlain. However, Salisbury's leadership was concerned with preventing too much reform. Curiously, this cautious approach ensured that it was his party that dominated the late nineteenth century.

In this chapter you will learn about:

▶ the impact of the 'Great Depression' on British politics
▶ Gladstone's 'Ministry of Troubles' (1880–85) and the third ministry of 1886
▶ Chamberlain's ideas on municipal socialism and imperialism
▶ Salisbury, Randolph Churchill and Tory democracy
▶ Liberal-Unionists and the decline of Liberalism
▶ Conservative domination in the late nineteenth century.

The 'Great Depression' years

In the years after 1870 there was a relative decline in British industry compared with other European powers and the USA. In Chapter 1, it was shown how S.B. Saul had refuted the idea of a Great Depression and certainly, by the standards of the slump of the 1930s, there was not the same degree of bad fortune. However, it was clear that there was a shift in the basis of Britain's trade, and that the industrialisation of other powers made it inevitable that Britain's primacy would be threatened.

The alleged loss of innovative spirit was off-set by new technologies
There has been much speculation that Britain was failing to produce the kind of entrepreneurs that had led the boom of the early industrial revolution. Nevertheless, there were many technical developments that boosted British trade. For example, four million tons of British shipping was powered by steam in 1885

whereas it had been only one million in 1870. The invention of the triple expansion engine in 1881, and the turbine engine in 1894, greatly reduced transportation time. In steel making, the Gilchrist-Thomas process (which eliminated phosphorus prevalent in British coal) improved the speed of manufacture. The first motor car appeared on British roads in 1894 (the Panhard) but railways continued to expand and arguably locomotives were entering their golden age. Telephones (Graham Bell 1875) and typewriters entered the business world to improve the efficiency of trade.

The formation of trusts
Until the late nineteenth century, most of Britain's industries were small family firms. However, towards the end of the century, the family business or partnership was giving way to the company. Shareholders, who had invested their life savings in a business, began to exert a little influence. Companies formed 'combines' or trusts to combat foreign competition. These groupings had the advantage of greater capital investment and could virtually dominate a particular commodity or, in extreme cases, actually hold a monopoly over one. The earliest trust in Britain was the Salt Union, formed in 1888. There were some calls for protectionism once other powers had erected tariff barriers to British goods, but the threat of dearer food was enough to deter the electorate in the period 1903–05 and Britain remained a free trade country until 1931.

British arable agriculture was ruined
The exploitation of the North American prairies was accelerated by the invention of the combine harvester. It was possible to produce grain in vast quantities at relatively little cost. Railways and steam shipping transported the wheat across the Atlantic, and, without protection, the British farmer could not compete. Governments were eager to satisfy the demand for cheap food from Britain's urban population, and wheat prices fell from 56s 9d a quarter in 1877 and never recovered to more than 44s. A series of poor harvests doubled the impact of lost earnings and many smaller farmers had to abandon agriculture. It is estimated that 100,000 left the land for the cities. Rents fell, and, as a result, land values went into decline. Wheatfields were reduced by half and the number of farm labourers fell by a third, even though the actual total population increased by 40% in the years 1870 and 1900. Refrigeration also made it possible to import cheap lamb from New Zealand and the first cargoes arrived in 1882.

Farming survived because of the increased domestic demand
The massive increase in Britain's population sustained a strong demand from the consumer for British goods. Meat, milk and vegetables were needed on an unprecedented scale and some farmers were able to shift the emphasis of production from grain to other products. Market gardening, especially in the London area, experienced a boom.

These economic changes cast doubt on Britain's future

Despite an unshakeable faith in the doctrine of free trade, there was some doubt about Britain's economic future. Joseph Chamberlain advocated an imperial free trade union, but argued that other countries should pay tariffs to trade with Britain and her Empire. The majority disagreed. The governments of the late Victorian era held to the belief that the economy should be unfettered, and, in the same way, there should be minimal government interference with the lives of individual. This *laissez faire* approach retarded the development of Britain's educational system since there was little emphasis on technical training. Schools tended to give a broad education focused on leadership and good character, primarily as preparation for rule in the Empire, but continental powers gave more prestige to a technical education.

Gladstone's 'Ministry of Troubles'

Perhaps unfairly Gladstone's second (1880–85) and third (1886) ministries are regarded as less successful than the first ministry (1868–74). However, despite Disraeli's charge in 1872 that the Liberals had 'run out of steam' and the fact that fewer reforms were passed, Gladstone was as proactive as before. Indeed, Liberalism, or rather Gladstone, had lost none of its/his energy especially when roused to fury. The Liberals achieved a great deal with the legislation that was passed. The problem was that Gladstone made a number of errors and aroused a great deal of anger amongst the British electorate. Foreign policy and affairs in Ireland were particularly damaging.

Gladstone's reforms included rights for women of property

The second ministry reforms do not look as abundant as those of the first ministry, but there are some pieces of legislation which seem more significant. The Married Women's Property Act (1882) addressed the issue of women's rights. Before the Act, women of property lost all right to their own goods on marriage. If her husband divorced her, she would lose everything. If her husband died, the goods would pass to the children, not necessarily to the wife (unless a will specified otherwise). For its time, the Married Woman's Property Act could be seen as a revolutionary measure, even if by today's standards its seems very modest. Once again, this reminds us of a key point concerning Victorian Britain: so much of what they did in the field of social reform was pioneering. Women were still disadvantaged in many areas of society, but middle-class women sought smaller families towards the end of the century in a quest to employ servants, pay school fees and thus to earn greater respectability. This freed more of their time for charitable work, assistance to the churches and participation in the arts. In education too, there were changes. The first women's colleges were established at Oxford, Cambridge (Girton 1873, Newnham 1876) and London (opened in 1878), although at first they were limited to study rather than qualifying for degrees.

Gladstone implemented greater democratisation
Perhaps the greatest achievements of the second ministry were in the realm of parliamentary reform. The Third Parliamentary Reform Act (1884) and the Redistribution of Seats Act (1885) ensured that the urban and rural working classes were given the vote under the same property qualifications and the drawing up of new constituency boundaries to take account of the growth of cities such as Birmingham and Glasgow. The franchise thus covered 5.7 million men in 1885. Unlike previous Acts, the 1884 legislation applied across the United Kingdom. The electorate of Ireland, which had been under-represented in parliament, gained the most from the Act; the number of voters increased from 220,000 to 740,000. The Irish Home Rule Party won 75% of the seats (85 out of 103) which considerably strengthened their position in the Commons. The Acts combined confirmed that Victorian politicians had to take account of working class interests to a greater extent, but they also had to appeal to all voters at a grass roots level. New political party associations sprang up, and new methods of canvassing votes. The 1872 Ballot Act which had been designed to give the voters the protection of a secret ballot was supplemented by the Corrupt and Illegal Practices Act (1883). Intimidation and bribery ('treating') carried stiff penalties. Strict limits were applied to how much candidates could spend on an election. Despite these measures, about 40% of adult males still had no vote.

Gladstone's assistance to the farmers was limited
Despite the hopes of the Farmers Alliance that Gladstone would come to the aid of the agricultural community, the depression in farming was not tackled adequately by the Liberals. In 1872, Joseph Arch had formed a National Agricultural Labourers Union but membership was devastated by the depression and the opposition of those landowners who feared that a labourers' strike would hold the country to ransom. The Abolition of the Malt Tax (1880) did away with a tax on barley producers and replaced it with a tax on beer. The Ground Game Act (1880) allowed labourers to hunt hares and rabbits without facing anti-poaching laws. The Agricultural Holdings Act (1883) made the Conservative legislation of 1875 compulsory. However, none of these Acts protected the farm labourer from eviction or destitution. Poverty could still lead to the workhouse. Protection of British agriculture was not entertained as a solution, so wedded were the Liberals to the idea of free trade. As a result, a lot of the old traditions and culture began to die away. Customs that had been repeated by generations from the middle ages, or perhaps even earlier, were gradually lost.

There was an absence of the great reforming zeal of the 1870s
Some of the Liberals' measures appealed only to their own supporters' narrow interests. The Burials Act (1880) was designed to appease Nonconformists because burials did not need a Church of England religious service. The Mundella Education Act (1880) also appealed to Liberal supporters because it made primary education compulsory. The Employers' Liability Act (1880) gave

employees financial compensation for injury at work, although in practice this
was hard to obtain.

Gladstone's domestic record was significant but inadequate

Against the background of the industrial and agricultural depressions, Gladstone's adherence to the traditions of *laissez faire* made him few friends amongst
those who were affected. Increasingly, he seemed to be out of step with the
aspirations of the people. He despised imperialism and made effective speeches to
condemn Disraeli's expansionist 'Forward Policy' as the excesses of 'Beaconsfield-
ism'. He had once argued that the Zulu or the Afghan refugee had as much right
to a home as anyone in England, but by the 1880s, Gladstone failed to
acknowledge the growing popularity of imperialism. His foreign policy, moreover,
appeared to represent the approach of a weak 'Little Englander' rather than a
'Great Briton'. Above all, it was his unpopular policy in Ireland which damaged
him (see Chapter 3). However, Gladstone's own verdict that this was the
'Ministry of Troubles' shows that he realised just how difficult it had been to
govern Britain in a period of immense change.

Gladstone's foreign policy was generally unpopular

In foreign policy, Gladstone misjudged events as he had done in the first ministry.
He evacuated Afghanistan in 1880 at the end of the Second Afghan War, really
following on from a policy initiated by the Conservatives. His liberal viceroy of
India, Lord Ripon, delayed the withdrawal to establish a firm government first.
Conservative critics felt that greater influence should have been retained over
Afghanistan, especially a permanent Resident (advisor) because that had been
the cause of the war in the first place. Gladstone instead offered to protect
Afghanistan's borders, but that would mean a war against Russia if there was a
border incident. Ripon went on to attempt some important reforms in India, but
this aroused criticism from the British community of the Raj. He cut defence
expenditure, reduced the Indian Army, and introduced the Ilbert Bill (an
attempt to bring equality before the law in India) but withdrew this measure after
protests by the Anglo-Indians (as the British in India were known).

Gladstone failed to uphold British prestige in southern Africa

In South Africa, the Transvaal revolted in 1880–81 against British control (which
had been established in 1877) and a British force was defeated at Majuba Hill
(February 1881). Gladstone refused to despatch a punitive expedition, instead
granting virtual independence at the Convention of Pretoria with a loose British
suzerainty (which was an acknowledgement that no other power should interfere
with the Transvaal, without consulting Britain). In 1884, London and Pretoria
established formal diplomatic relations without mentioning suzerainty which led
to confusion about Transvaal's status in the 1890s. However, the most important
impact in 1881 was at home where Gladstone was viewed as a weak statesman
because of his concessions to the Transvaal.

Gladstone wanted to judge each case on its own merits
The incidents in Afghanistan and South Africa prove Gladstone was opposed to imperialism and demonstrate his determination to fulfil the election pledges of the Midlothian Campaign (1879–80). He was filled with a deep sense of moral righteousness and a feeling that individual small nations had a right to self rule. This was a long development for Gladstone. He saw Home Rule in action in Norway, and he had seen the evils of tyrannical government in Naples in the 1850s. He had been repelled by the excesses of the Ottoman Empire against the smaller nationalities of the Balkans and he had been enraptured by the process of Italian unification. It is not surprising that in the 1880s he was slowly considering the idea of self-government for Ireland. There is a danger this argument can go too far, of course. Gladstone did little to dismantle the Empire, bar the withdrawal of garrisons in the 'white' colonies, and Gladstone actually extended British imperial rule by occupying Egypt in 1882 and annexing Bechuanaland in 1884–85.

The occupation of Egypt (1882) followed its financial collapse
Egypt had been plagued by financial mismanagement for decades. Although the *fellahin* (peasantry) paid high taxes, officials at every level of the administration took a considerable share for themselves. In 1876, the Khedive was declared bankrupt and a Public Debt Commission was established to handle foreign investments. By 1878, this arrangement had failed and a British and a French official were appointed to run the fiscal side of the Egyptian government. However, it was clear that, without a major overhaul of the entire corrupt system, this too would fail. In the 1880 Law of Liquidation, it was decreed that 60% of Egypt's revenue would have to be allocated to pay off foreign debt. In the unrest which followed, Arabi Pasha, a colonel of the Egyptian army launched a *coup d'état* in 1881. Arabi was determined to evict the foreign financiers from the country. Britain and France aimed for joint action against the *coup*, but Leon Gambetta's government fell from power in January 1882 and the French refused to co-operate further. A naval demonstration was planned in the hope that a show of force would be enough to persuade Arabi to negotiate. However, Arabi began to reinforce the coastal defences of the port of Alexandria. Admiral Seymour, the British squadron commander, knew that the guns in the forts there posed a considerable threat to his fleet. Consequently, Alexandria was bombarded on 11 July 1882.

Gladstone was drawn into the conflict in Egypt
Anti-European riots had resulted in the deaths of many civilians in Alexandria in June 1882, so Seymour's naval bombardment meant that protection against reprisals was inevitable. Gladstone felt there was a moral necessity to prevent anarchy, bloodshed and disorder, and he knew that British investments, and the Suez Canal, were at risk if he did not act. It could be argued that Gladstone was forced to strike either by Joseph Chamberlain, who was a persuasive imperialist ('Pushful Joe'), or by the Navy; this is the view of historian M.E. Chamberlain.

Nevertheless, it was Gladstone who took the decision, however reluctantly, and he felt equally compelled to remain in Egypt until stable government and financial security for the Egyptians could be guaranteed, even though he had initially hoped for a 'rescue and retire' operation. General Sir Garnet Wolseley led the British Expeditionary Force into Egypt and he defeated the main field army of Arabi Pasha in one decisive engagement at Tel El Kebir. Britain thus found itself in possession of Egypt.

The British control of Egypt had mixed success
Evelyn Baring, later Lord Cromer, was appointed Consul-General of Egypt in 1883 and he virtually ruled the country for 24 years. In this period he improved cultivation and irrigation and modernised the state bureaucracy, eliminating many of the old abuses in the process. He organised military reforms using British officers. Financially, Egypt recovered from bankruptcy but there was concern that a rapid withdrawal would leave the country exposed to fresh uprisings. In 1884, Gladstone appealed to the other European powers for an international loan and 'joint control'. He was eager to revive the old idea of a Concert of Europe, particularly as he wanted to avoid the charge of British unilateral action and aggression. In this he failed. Lord Salisbury summed up the irony in 1885 when he announced: 'Gladstone has succeeded in uniting Europe – against Britain'.

Gladstone was blamed for the death of the popular General Gordon
By occupying Egypt, Gladstone also became responsible for the safety of the Egyptians who faced the revolt of the former Egyptian colony, Sudan. Mohammed Ahmad, the *Mahdi* (messiah), called on the Sudanese to fight the Egyptians and the British. Egyptian forces under Generals Hicks and Baker made little progress so Gladstone ordered General Charles Gordon to evacuate the Sudan altogether (1884). Hoping for a change of government, Gordon set out to defend Khartoum (Sudan's capital) against the *Mahdi*. Gladstone refused to send a relief force to rescue Gordon until public pressure mounted against him. Wolseley's relieving army arrived two days too late. The death of Gordon was Gladstone's nadir; he was abused by the general public and the Queen sent a reprimand.

Britain's international weakness was only one aspect in Gladstone's defeat
Within weeks another crisis exploded as Britain's protected state, Afghanistan, was attacked by the Russians at Penjdeh (1885), provoking a war scare. At that moment Bismarck, the German Chancellor, was hostile to Britain, and the Russians, Austrians and Germans acted together against Britain. This meant that Britain's traditional domination of the eastern Mediterranean was in doubt. With French colonial antagonism also growing, Britain was diplomatically isolated. It may have been this public anger at Britain's international weakness that finally determined the election result that November, but there was a combination of factors which stemmed from a mediocre domestic record too. In the end it came

down to the relative strengths of the parties in the House of Commons. The Conservatives and Liberals were fairly evenly matched, and the Irish MPs held the balance of power. The second ministry collapsed in June 1885, when Irish MPs deserted the Liberals.

Gladstone's third ministry (1886) ended in the split of the Liberal Party
Gladstone's third ministry was short lived and consisted entirely of an attempt to introduce the first Home Rule Bill (see Chapter 3). Chamberlain had urged Gladstone to avoid the Irish issue or at least acknowledge the importance of social reform in the election of 1885, but Gladstone would not be deterred. Chamberlain therefore released his own manifesto for reform known as the 'unauthorised programme'. This promised further improvements in the living and working conditions of the people. Gladstone forged ahead with a Home Rule Bill because he was dependent on the Irish Home Rulers to stay in power, but Chamberlain could not accept the devolution of the United Kingdom. He felt that the break-up of the United Kingdom was possible, and that, in turn, there was a risk that the Empire would also break apart. Chamberlain voted against the Bill with 92 other Liberals, some of whom were radicals, but the rest were Whigs (the right wing of the Party). The Liberal Party split from that moment. Yet Gladstone had also alienated Joe Chamberlain, who was, without doubt, one of the most talented members of the Liberal Party. 1886 marked the beginning of a period of decline in the party, and, but for one short ministry in 1892–5, they were out of office for 16 years.

Chamberlain's ideas on municipal socialism and imperialism

Municipal socialism was a concept of civic improvements
Chamberlain had begun his career as a screw manufacturer, but he was an energetic man, eager to do something to improve his home town of Birmingham. He became mayor between 1873 and 1876, and then a Liberal MP, serving as President of the Board of Trade in Gladstone's second ministry of 1880–6. He held this post until he split from the Liberal Party over Home Rule. As mayor he had established a reputation as a 'radical' reformer. Under his direction the Birmingham Council bought up the gas and water companies, expanded them and carried out a series of improvements. A new hospital was built, a drainage board established, streets were paved, lighting set up, six parks were created, and a national conference was established to set an example for other cities. Ninety acres of slums were demolished, using Disraeli's legislation of 1875 and replaced with the commercially orientated Corporation Street, business areas and new residential areas. New libraries and art galleries followed, and, in 1900, Birmingham University was established. The clock tower there is still called 'Old Joe' in his memory. This process of city reform was called 'municipal socialism'.

Chamberlain contributed to the Liberal Party

Chamberlain set up the Birmingham Liberal Association which enabled him to become elected. He gave £1,000 to set up the Birmingham Education League (which later developed into the National League) and campaigned for free, compulsory education. He formed the National Liberal Federation in 1877 calling for further reforms for the working classes, and he reorganised the party at grass roots level. He was nicknamed 'radical Joe'. He pushed for and got the Third Parliamentary Reform Act in 1884. Chamberlain was something of a visionary. He could see the direction British politics was taking and embraced greater democratisation. However, he fell foul of Gladstone in 1885 for releasing the 'unauthorised programme' (he was angry with Gladstone's emphasis on Ireland at the expense of social reforms which had been the hallmark of earlier Liberal administrations) but the programme probably helped the Liberals in the election of November 1885. He had promoted the idea of 'Three Acres and a Cow'; giving small holdings to farm labourers hit by the agricultural depression. He called for the payment of MPs so that ordinary folk could sit in Parliament. He wanted a graduated income tax and the establishment of County Councils. Significantly he called for pensions and sickness insurance, measures that would eventually be passed in the 1900s.

Chamberlain had genuine motives for opposing Home Rule

Despite the accusation that Chamberlain split the Liberals to seize the leadership for himself, there is no evidence of this. He justified his split from Gladstone in 1886 by arguing that the trade depression that was hitting Britain in the 1880s could be solved by a development of the Empire as a trading organisation. Gladstone's Home Rule programme threatened to dismantle the Empire, rather than strengthen it. Chamberlain was probably influenced by the ideas of men like Professor Seeley (Cambridge University) who had written in 1883 that the future would be dominated by great Empires rather than small nations. As a radical, Chamberlain also believed that Britain could benefit the subject peoples of the Empire. This genuine commitment to the Empire was evident when he refused the job of Chancellor of the Exchequer in 1895 (in a Conservative government) and took up the unpopular post of Colonial Secretary instead.

Chamberlain held on to a radical agenda

Chamberlain continued to press for reforms and helped the Conservatives to frame the Workman's Compensation Act of 1897. Although seamen, servants and agricultural labourers were excluded, they were eventually assisted by legislation in 1908. Chamberlain continued to advocate the merits of Old Age Pensions and the legislation was probably only delayed by the fact that no funds were available after the expensive Boer War of 1899–1902.

Chamberlain was proactive as Colonial Secretary

He negotiated successfully during the Venezuela dispute when America had virtually threatened war in 1895. Visiting the USA, he persuaded them to accept the British claim to defend British Guiana and its claimed territory. Venezuela, which America had backed, was forced to submit its objections to international arbitration and lost.

Chamberlain sanctioned a number of imperial actions

In 1896, Chamberlain despatched General Wolseley to pacify the Ashanti raiders on the Gold Coast. They were defeated and British control was re-established. The following year, Chamberlain ordered the formation of a defence force in Nigeria (West African Frontier Force) in response to a French seizure of villages along a disputed border with Dahomey. The French compromised and a settled border was achieved in June 1898. The Sudan, which had been in a state of unrest since 1884, was reconquered by British forces under Kitchener in 1898. The Fashoda Incident, where French troops tried to claim possession of southern Sudan, was handled by Chamberlain and, once again, he obtained a peaceful settlement. In China, Chamberlain ordered the seizure of the port of Wei Hei Wei in response to a German annexation of Kiaochow, in order to 'safeguard Britain's interests'. The port was in fact leased from the Chinese and would be returned when the lease expired. This was in contrast to the German action and was in keeping with previous arrangements with China.

Chamberlain worked hard on improvements to the Empire

Chamberlain wanted to see the improvement of the Empire that already existed. He encouraged the formation of joint stock companies in this venture. Government money was spent on projects such as the Uganda railway, harbours in Jamaica, irrigation and railways in Cyprus, and railways in Lagos and Sierra Leone. He set up the School of Tropical Medicine to investigate and prevent diseases in the Empire. He called a colonial conference in 1897 to discuss the idea of imperial consolidation, planning the meeting to coincide with the Queen's jubilee celebrations. Chamberlain also promoted the concept of 'imperial preference'. This was the establishment of a free trade customs union within the British Empire, but the establishment of protective tariffs against all non-Empire countries. However, the white dominions refused to co-operate for fear of damaging their own countries' economies and they again refused in 1902, despite co-operation in the Boer War.

Chamberlain became embroiled in events in South Africa

Cecil Rhodes, the diamond tycoon from Cape Colony, approached Chamberlain for permission to use British territory (Bechuanaland) to launch a rebellion against the government of the Transvaal. Chamberlain agreed because he was eager to see South Africa confederated under the British flag. However, the ill-fated Jameson Raid (December 1895) was an embarrassing failure for Chamberlain. The Transvaal suspected the British government's connivance, despite Chamberlain's claim that he had had nothing to do with Rhodes' plan. In

1899, Alfred Milner, the British High Commissioner of Cape Colony, engineered a war against the Transvaal because its government imposed heavy taxation on the gold-mining operations around Johannesburg and denied political rights to the predominantly British workforce there. Chamberlain genuinely felt that this was what the war was about, but Milner concealed his intrigues from the Colonial Secretary in London. The South African War (or Boer War as it was known) broke out in 1899 and lasted until 1902.

Chamberlain's promising career ended with a split in the Conservatives

Chamberlain's interest in developing the Empire at first appears to be inconsistent with his early radicalism. However, Chamberlain saw the Empire as a great opportunity for British manufacturers and aimed for a mutually beneficial relationship between the colonies and the metropole. Raw materials would pour into Britain for manufacture, and the colonies would enjoy the fruits of British products. The circulation of trade inside this vast market would be protected by tariffs and provide cheap food and consumer goods. Exposure to competition from other European countries was detrimental in Chamberlain's world-view. To raise awareness of the growing European threat and to further promote the idea of an imperial customs union he launched the tariff reform campaign in Britain in 1903. Although Balfour, the Premier, never denounced it, or supported it, it split the Conservatives and contributed towards the election defeat of 1905. Chamberlain suffered a stroke in 1906 and, without recovering his health, he died in 1914.

Salisbury, Randolph Churchill and Tory democracy

Lord Salisbury believed in self-help

Robert Cecil, 3rd Marquis of Salisbury, served as Indian Secretary and Foreign Secretary before becoming Prime Minister in 1885. He hardly adopted a philosophy for the Conservative Party at all during his years of leadership, since he embodied the Party values in himself. He was tall and imposing, his character exuded calm. He was wealthy and a patrician. These values seemed to embody the very stability of late Victorian Britain. He was Britain's last aristocratic Prime Minister. Salisbury's domestic aims were to preserve and extend individual freedom, and promote self-help and preserve the established institutions. His views on self-help were best summed up when he said: 'No men ever rise to any permanent improvement in their condition of body or of mind except by relying on their own personal efforts.' However, this was not from any indifference to the conditions of the ordinary citizen, Salisbury was willing to create the conditions for self help. Above all, he appears to have shared the Conservative idea that wealth, generated by industry (both at a personal and national level), would seep down to the masses. The duty of government was therefore to interfere as little as possible with this. This may explain his desire to see greater devolution of government by creating County and District Councils (1888 and 1894). Nevertheless, he was uncertain of the consequences of democracy. It seemed inconceivable to him that a working-class man could understand the great delicacy and complexity of foreign policy. Indeed, he hardly trusted his own class with this task and combined the duties of Foreign Secretary *and* Prime Minister. He was highly industrious as a result, often locking himself away for hours to study a particular problem.

Salisbury's primary interest was in foreign affairs

He wanted to avoid foreign commitments to other powers which might embroil Britain in a war, so he made no alliances. He regarded war as 'the supreme evil' and saw that it would only damage British trade. However, he was prepared to support colonial wars which served Britain's interests. He believed in Britain's ability to defend herself, despite some pessimistic utterances on the subject, and went to some lengths to ensure this (including a review of Britain's world position in the Defence Committee of 1895, and by the expansion of the Royal Navy). He aimed to avoid conflict by international co-operation between the world's leaders. This was not to be done by a Concert of Europe, but through 'understandings' with other powers. Salisbury's foreign policy has sometimes been described as a period of 'splendid isolation' for Britain.

Salisbury wanted to avoid confrontation in Ireland

Salisbury was deeply sceptical of what he regarded as the rabble-rousing tactics of Randolph Churchill or Gladstone, and uncomfortable with Liberal policies in Ireland. He felt the role of his party was to defend Britain from radicalism. He wanted to resolve the violence which Gladstone had generated, by non-controversial economic and social reform, supported by firm government by Balfour, the Chief Secretary in Ireland. In the circumstances, this was less an ideological response than a practical solution (see Chapter 3). He once remarked, on changes in British society and politics, 'Whatever happens will be for the worse, and therefore it is in our interest that as little should happen as possible.' This is a rather self-effacing criticism of his record both in Britain and in Ireland, for the period of his ministries was remarkable calm despite the changes taking place.

Lord Randolph Churchill was a radical of the Conservative Party

Randolph Churchill was a Conservative Party politician eager to revive the approach of Disraeli. He referred to the merits of Tory democracy, the Conservatives' record of parliamentary reform, as a means to combat the Liberals. He advocated social reforms on the same scale as Disraeli's second ministry in order to turn the Conservatives into a truly popular party. He was also an outspoken critic of members of his own party. When, during a debate about the two greatest parties of the country, the Irish Home Rulers had claimed that there were, in fact, three great parties. Churchill called out, half in jest, that there were four, that is, himself. He, and his three closest colleagues were referred to as the 'Fourth Party', or the 'Ginger Group'. They became infamous for their goading attacks on Gladstone and Sir Stafford Northcote.

Churchill had attracted Irish support in 1885
Churchill attracted the support of Irish MPs when he seemed to promise reforms for Ireland at a time when the Liberals appeared to have faltered in concessions after the Land War of 1882. The switch of Irish allegiances brought down Gladstone's government and kept them out of office in the November 1885 election. Gladstone's offer of Home Rule destroyed the Conservative-Irish alliance. However, the split of the Liberals in 1886 over the first Home Rule Bill returned the Conservatives with a majority of 40, supported by 78 Liberal-Unionists (anti-Home Rule) and Irish Unionists.

Churchill suggested a radical programme as Chancellor of the Exchequer
There was great hope of change when the new Conservative Government was formed. The prospects for social reforms were summed up by Churchill's speech at Dartford (October 1886). He looked forward to: improvements in public health, better housing, compulsory national insurance, small holdings for agricultural labourers, reforms of parliamentary procedure, the provision of parks and open spaces, the establishment of libraries and art galleries for the general public, the opening of museums, and the construction of public baths and wash houses. He was appointed Chancellor of the Exchequer in August 1886 and to raise money for these schemes, he advocated death duties, and house duty, both of which were attacks on those with property. However, he also wanted a reduction of income tax, a reduction of tea and tobacco duty, and cuts in defence spending. W.H. Smith (the Minister of War) objected and Salisbury supported Smith because of Britain's diplomatic isolation. Nevertheless, it wasn't just the necessities of defence; Salisbury was concerned about the divisions it could arouse in the party. Churchill resigned just before Christmas 1886 in a bluff that failed; he thought Salisbury wouldn't let him go. Groschen became Chancellor, and Churchill fell ill. He died in 1895, aged only 45.

Conservative reforms made an attempt to address issues facing the people
Conservative reforms included the Labourers Allotments Act (1887) which empowered local authorities to buy land for urban workers so that they could 'elevate themselves into positions of manly independence by their industry'. The Act was disappointing because few authorities took up the opportunity. The Mines Regulation Act (1887) gave the miners greater legal protection at work, whilst the Tithe Act (1890) made it possible for the owner of a property, not the occupier, to pay a traditional tithe payment to the church. The property of labourers who lived in rented accommodation was therefore protected. In education, the Cross Commission led to the Fee Grant Act (1891) which abolished fees in primary education. The Factory Act (1891) raised the minimum age for child labour to eleven and laid down the maximum working days for women as twelve hours (with one and a half hours for meals).

The most far-reaching changes were in local government

The Local Government Act (1888) swept away a collection of 27,000 boards covering a myriad of different areas of administration, from drainage to street lighting. Sixty-two elected County Councils replaced the old boards and they took over many of the tasks previously carried out by the appointed JPs (Justices of the Peace). Sixty towns (over 50,000 people) were converted into County Boroughs with the same powers as the County Councils. London was divided into 28 Metropolitan Boroughs under the control of the London County Council. Strikingly, for the first time, unmarried women were allowed to vote on these councils. These measures represented a great democratisation of Britain. The rural labourers given the vote in 1884 had the chance to participate in the election of the local authority in their area. This raises a question about Salisbury, who often lamented the growth of democracy. Did he in fact calculate that rural voters would be conservative? Or did he see this step as inevitable and therefore better carried out by his own party than his opponents? Alternatively, the local government reforms could be seen as the fulfilment of the ideas of Tory Democracy advocated by Churchill.

Poverty in Britain remained unresolved

Despite the pride Britons felt in their Empire, there was a shocking degree of poverty for many people in Britain itself. Living conditions remained particularly poor for the least well off, despite housing legislation in the 1870s. For some, wages were inadequate to sustain good health. By 1900, it was estimated that as many as one third of Britons were at or below the poverty line. In 1886 there were riots in the West End of London when poorer workers launched an angry protest, and in 1889 a strike by dockers attracted much sympathy when it was revealed their diet at times consisted of soup and fish remains. During the strike, other unions' members contributed money to support the dock workers. A considerable sum was sent by the Australian unions. After four weeks, the dock owners gave way. Despite this industrial action, Salisbury still felt that self-help, not state intervention, was the answer. He was, in fact, typical of the time in this respect. The individual's enterprise was respected, but at the same time, class barriers often made it difficult to 'get on'. It was noticeable how these social rules were less valid in the colonies, an area perfect for the enterprise of determined men.

Liberal-Unionists and the decline of Liberalism

Gladstone's fourth ministry faltered over Ireland

The last Liberal administration of the nineteenth century was short lived and epitomised the problems the Party faced. The Conservatives still outnumbered the Liberals in the election of 1892, but the Liberal-Unionists and the Conservatives were smaller than the Gladstone-Irish Nationalist combination. Gladstone was therefore dependent on the Irish to stay in power and this made it inevitable that he would try to introduce a Home Rule Bill. Nevertheless, he passionately pursued his goal of granting Ireland devolution for quite genuine reasons; he really believed that Irishmen must settle their own difficulties. He presented a second Bill in February 1893. This was quite out of step with the concept of imperial consolidation, but in keeping with the granting of dominion status to Canada, Australia and New Zealand. It passed through the Commons with Irish support. The Lords, still the most important body of Parliament until the 1900s, rejected it.

Gladstone hoped the 'Newcastle Programme' would be popular

The Liberal manifesto of 1892 offered a package of reforms (the 'Newcastle Programme'). These included: elections every three years, allotments for labourers, district and parish councils, payments for MPs (allowing working men to serve in parliament where previously a private income was essential), and new liabilities for employers if workers fell ill or were injured at work. However, there is little evidence that the electorate voted positively for this programme. When the Liberals came to power, their most important reform was the Local Government Act (1894). This was a refinement on the Act of 1888, which gave working-class people more power at local level. The county councils had too much to process, so the 1894 Act sub-divided counties into rural and urban districts with their own councils. Parishes in the countryside also got an administration of their own. Married women were allowed to vote. Both married and unmarried women were permitted to stand for election. This was the first step in the long road towards women's suffrage.

Gladstone resigned in March 1894

Gladstone lost the support of his colleagues over the Naval Estimates, allocating sums to the Royal Navy for defence. The world had changed from Gladstone's early career, and Britain's naval supremacy could no longer be taken for granted. Britain was dangerously isolated and Gladstone's proposal to cut defence spending (in line with his ideas on retrenchment) was regarded as irresponsible. Gladstone resigned as he had sometimes threatened to do in the past, after pressure from his colleagues. His resignation was accepted. He retired, and died in 1898. Without Gladstone at the helm, the Liberals were without a leader who could hold the Party together.

Lord Rosebery, Gladstone's successor, miscalculated

Rosebery was an aristocratic Liberal who had little experience in party management. His Chancellor, Harcourt, managed to introduce death duties in his budget but all other Liberal bills were rejected by the House of Lords. The justification given by this Conservative-dominated body was that the Liberal majority was to small to warrant a mandate from the people. Rosebery resigned, hoping the public would turn against the Lords. He miscalculated. The Liberals were defeated in the 1895 election, returning with only 177 seats against the

Conservatives' 340 and their 71 Liberal-Unionist supporters. The Irish were divided over Parnell's conduct, but even their 83 members could make no difference to the Conservatives' majority.

Were the Liberals in decline?

The fortunes of the Liberals in the last decades of the nineteenth century were at a low ebb. They were divided over Ireland, unable to inspire the public with their social reform programmes, unable to by-pass the House of Lords which had rejected their bills, and they hadn't produced an effective successor to Gladstone as leader. Their radicalism also alarmed many traditional Liberal supporters in the middle classes. In the mid-nineteenth century, the middle classes had regarded the Liberals as their champions in the struggle against the supremacy of the aristocracy. Protectionism had been abolished, the civil service and the highest ranks of government had been opened up to middle-class men. Parliamentary reform in the 1860s had granted the vote to men with modest amounts of property. However, the prospect of reforms which enfranchised the ill-educated, empowered the trades unions or which favoured the men without property did not enamour the middle classes. They grew concerned about the rise of militant socialism on the continent. They began to have more in common with the Conservatives' agenda.

Conservative domination at the end of the nineteenth century

The Conservatives dominated the period between 1886 and 1905. This seems surprising when one considers that the franchise had been extended in 1867 and 1884 to include more working men. The Conservatives, traditionally the party of the aristocracy and the propertied, did not seem to be a party that could command the support of working-class men. Yet the election results of the period indicate that the working classes were not voting on simple class lines or the Liberals would have done well. In fact, voters could be swayed by a variety of issues and ideas, rather than class solidarity. The most popular Conservative idea was the promotion of the British Empire. Working men, already strongly patriotic (often for Britain rather than England, Wales or Scotland), were frequently inspired by the deeds of imperial figures. Yet this should not be overemphasised. Working men also wanted to see tangible improvements to their lives in economic terms. On the whole (although dependent on the employment and the region) wages improved in the last decade of the nineteenth century.

The relative importance of factors in explaining Conservative domination

The allegiance of the middle classes in England began to shift from the Liberals to the Conservatives at the end of the nineteenth century. Since they dwelt in large town houses, or villas, the change was known as 'Villa Toryism'. This shift, essentially a negative one because of the fear of radicalism, can be compared with the positive attraction of the Conservatives policies: an absence of reform at home, and an active imperial policy overseas. Both factors perhaps worked together to produce a change in voting behaviour. In Scotland and Wales, Liberal support remained strong. Disestablishment of the Anglican Church was desired on the 'Celtic fringe' because there was such a high proportion of Nonconformists and because of the lead shown in Ireland. The Conservatives benefited in a small way from 'plural voting', where men with property in more than one constituency were eligible for a vote in each location. This advantage should not be exaggerated since it affected relatively few people. The domination of the House of Lords was of greater consequence because it allowed them the chance to defeat Liberal bills, but ensure the passage of Conservative ones.

The Conservative Party ran into problems in the new century
Balfour took over in 1900 as Salisbury fell ill, but he was not a strong leader. He was the natural choice because he was the nephew of Salisbury, but he passed only a few measures (such as the Licensing Act, the 1902 Education Act and land reform for Ireland – see Chapter 6). He won the election of 1900 as Britain fought the Boer War (the so-called 'khaki election', named after the colour of the soldiers' uniforms) which cashed in on the strong patriotic feelings of the public, but he failed to disassociate the Conservatives from the Tariff Reform Campaign run by Joe Chamberlain. This campaign advocated a return to protectionism which led to Liberal accusations that food would become more expensive. The Conservatives suffered a massive defeat in 1905.

Conclusions: there were major setbacks for the Liberals
Gladstone claimed that the second ministry was the 'Ministry of Troubles', and we know that the third ministry was a disaster for the Liberals since the Home Rule Bill split the Party. The fourth ministry was a personal setback for Gladstone, because his ideas were regarded as out of date and he was accused of being out of touch. He had been effective in opposition, and he had been a prudent chancellor, but his performance in the ministries was ultimately marred by failure to produce the result he desired in Ireland. Perhaps Gladstone's successes can be measured in terms of his contribution to the British people through his social reforms. Alternatively, it could have been the achievement of holding the Liberals together for so long. What had changed in 1895, however, was the permanent defection of Liberal-Unionists.

There were divisions in the Party which were not easily resolved
The Liberals were defeated for several reasons: they relied on Irish Nationalist support, the party was split from 1886 and lost two leading men in Lord Hartington and Joseph Chamberlain, the 1893 Home Rule Bill was defeated and there didn't seem to be a focus once Gladstone had resigned. They relied on the Welsh and Scottish voters because they had lost a great deal of working-class and middle-class support in England. Gladstone's successors failed to lead effectively.

Rosebery resigned after the defeat of 1895, and was replaced by Harcourt. He was replaced in 1898 by Henry Campbell-Bannerman (who was largely an unknown in politics). Their agenda was unclear. D.A Hamer argued that 'Sectionalism re-emerged, rampant and uncontrollable'. Paul Adelman, in *Gladstone, Disraeli and later Victorian Politics* (1983), described a reversion to 'faddism' where each Liberal MP pursued his own interests, such as temperance, or, as in the case of Rosebery, the desire to develop the Empire. Some Welsh MPs wanted the disestablishment of the Church of England in Wales.

Conservative strength or Liberal weakness?

It could be argued that it was not so much the strength of Conservatives as the weakness of the Liberals that left the Conservative-Unionists (as they styled themselves in the 1890s) in power for so long. However, without either side really addressing the issues of poverty and further social reform then discontent was bound to emerge. What offset the demand for reform may have been the popularity of imperialism, but it may have also been the improvement in wages, the economic stability of the 1890s and the shift in support from the middle classes to the Conservatives.

Tutorial

Progress questions

1. Which was Gladstone's most successful ministry?

2. How consistent were Chamberlain's ideas of radicalism and imperialism?

3. What was Salisbury's guiding philosophy?

4. Why did the Conservatives dominate the late nineteenth century?

Seminar discussion

1. Which was the most important in determining voting behaviour in this period: class, imperialism, economic conditions or social reform?

2. Were the Liberals in decline between 1886 and 1906, and does *this* explain the Conservatives' domination?

Practical assignment

1. List the four main personalities of this period: Chamberlain, Salisbury, Gladstone and Churchill. Annotate their main achievements and their failures to the list.

2. List and assess the main changes in British society under the following headings: economy, the unity of the United Kingdom, popular imperialism, democratisation and civil unrest.

Study tips

1. Check that you know what was changing in British society and what the consequences were.

2. Try to recall each of the main players in the period, and their ideas. Notice how they take account of the greater degree of democracy in Britain. Note the growing sense of unease about popular politics and radicalism. Be prepared to explain these reactions.

5

Foreign and Imperial Policies, 1880–1902

One-minute summary – The last twenty years of the nineteenth century was marked by the rapid industrial growth of the European powers, especially Germany, and the USA. Britain's economic pre-eminence, which had arisen from her early industrialisation, was threatened by this development. Nevertheless, Britain still retained both a powerful navy and an army augmented by the manpower of its myriad imperial possessions. Britain was also still a leading industrial nation and its commerce was based on the principle of free trade. Her diplomatic isolation, whether deliberate (because of these strengths) or accidental, is the subject of some controversy. So too, is the question of Britain's motives for the rapid imperial expansion in this period. The last years of the century appear to have been a transition in the balance of military and economic power away from Britain towards the continental powers. When Britain engaged in an extensive war in South Africa, the weaknesses of her imperial facade were exposed. The situation demonstrated the need for a comprehensive review of Britain's commitments and the requirements of imperial defence against potential European enemies.

In this chapter you will learn about:

▶ British interests and naval power
▶ British foreign policy and the European Powers: splendid isolation
▶ foreign policy, 1886–1899
▶ the British Empire: the scramble for Africa, British rule in Asia, and the dominions
▶ the South African War, 1899–1902
▶ historical controversies about the British Empire and foreign policy.

British interests and naval power

The aims of British foreign policy

Foreign policy refers to Britain's relations with other European powers. The aims of foreign policy were to avoid war and to protect Britain's interests. War was 'the supreme evil' (Salisbury) and British Foreign Secretaries wanted to maintain peace, both for humanitarian reasons and for the promotion of British trade which could suffer as a result of war. The protection of Britain's interests meant, primarily, the defence of the United Kingdom, then the defence of the Empire, defence of its trade, and the maintenance of British prestige (which was the means by which Britain had a reputation of being powerful and therefore was a way to avoid a war with another European power). Salisbury spoke of the need 'to uphold

England's honour steadily and fearlessly and always be prone to let action go along with words rather than to let it lag behind them'. However he also seemed to want to avoid any changes in British foreign policy and claimed to want to 'drift lazily downstream, putting out occasional boathooks to stave off disaster'. Paul Kennedy criticised this policy for its lack of initiative and conservatism for it left Britain isolated.

Naval power
In the first half of the nineteenth century, Britannia certainly ruled the waves. The Royal Navy was vast, dwarfing other European powers. Besides its battleships there was a great armada of gunboats and smaller vessels. In addition, there was a vast merchant marine, plying between the colonies, Europe and the Americas. British colonies were always under the coastal supervision of Royal Naval vessels and the appearance of even a modest flotilla could deter local resistance. Colonial stations relied on the swift reinforcement of troops by the Royal Navy, and amphibious operations were conducted several times during the nineteenth century. In the Crimean War (1853–56), the navy bombarded the Russians in the Baltic, raided the Black Sea installations, blockaded Sevastopol and landed the British Army first at Varna and then at Eupatoria Bay on the Crimean Peninsula. These operations were only possible because of naval supremacy. In 1875, 241 ships were in commission of which 20 were ships of the line, and personnel totalled 34,000. Fifty-two of these vessels were in home waters, 18 in the Mediterranean, 22 in Chinese waters, 13 in South East Asia and 15 in North America and the West Indies, with the rest divided between the Cape, South America, Australasia and a collection of naval stations. Their duties included combating piracy in the Red Sea, protecting missionaries and traders, anti-slave trade patrols, debt collection in South America, as well as support for army operations in Egypt, China, or on the Nile. In 1898, the number of commissioned vessels was 287, but 52 of them were battleships. Personnel had increased to 97,000, but other than the Mediterranean and Home fleet, the distribution of strength was not vastly altered. Thirty-eight vessels patrolled the Mediterranean, but the home defence contingent had been reduced to 15, albeit with a greater number of battleships.

The Merchant Navy was a vital lifeline to British prosperity
One of the Royal Navy's key roles was the protection of the vast merchant marine which brought in some £200 million every year, and which was regarded as the lifeline of Britain's future prosperity. There was even a significant shift in the source of Britain's foodstuffs, for whilst in the 1830s 90% of Britain's food was grown at home, by the turn of the century a third was imported. Between 1857 and 1875, annual corn imports rose from £19.4 million to £51.7 million, and meat rose from £3.5 million to £13.8 million. There was a need to protect British trade, not just for the nation's wealth, but for the country's survival. Britain's merchant fleet was the largest in the world, and operated across the globe, and as

such, demanded from the Royal Navy an ability to respond whatever the circumstances, with greater strength. Added to this demand was a desire to continue to be the largest navy in the world as a symbol of Britain's power and prestige.

The end of undisputed British naval supremacy?

According to Paul Kennedy, the era of inexpensive naval supremacy which the British had enjoyed for most of the nineteenth century came to an abrupt end in 1884. The revelation of a French shipbuilding programme that threatened Britain led to popular pressure for action, and Gladstone, beleaguered already by the setbacks to his policy in Egypt and the Sudan, was forced to spend an extra £3.1 million on warships, and a further £2.1 million on naval ordnance and coaling stations. In 1888, Salisbury was also faced by public pressure for greater expenditure in light of the growth of French and Russian fleets. Yet, whilst Kennedy asserts that this was part of a long-term decline in Britain's industrial strength, mixed with British complacency and a greater industrial capacity by other European powers, the rethink of British naval strategy and imperial defence was inevitable. There was, however, a reluctance to see that its Crimean strategy was no longer guaranteed success. Nevertheless, the Royal Navy remained the world's largest fleet until the 1930s.

The Eastern Mediterranean was a focus of concern

British strategy in the Near East was concerned with the protection of the Suez Canal and the trade routes to the East. There was concern that Russia's fleet in the Black Sea posed a threat to the sea lanes of the region. Britain had relied on the co-operation of the Ottoman Empire, but Gladstone had been an outspoken critic of Turkey which he regarded as incapable of humanitarian reform. He was scornful of the notion that the defence of Turkey was the only bulwark against Russian domination of the Balkans, and advocated the recourse to reasoned diplomacy and international co-operation in a revived Concert of Europe. After the invasion of Egypt (1882), a former vassal of the Ottoman Empire, Britain's deteriorating relations with the Sultan never really recovered, and Salisbury was sceptical of any improvement. By 1897, with the outbreak of rebellion in Armenia, and the Greco-Turkish War, Britain was clearly no longer aligned with the Ottomans.

The Admiralty was pessimistic

In 1892, Admiral C. Bridge, the Director of Naval Intelligence, informed the Cabinet of its options in the event of a Russian attack on Constantinople. Bridge feared that if the Russians seized Constantinople, they would constitute a direct threat to the Suez Canal, and limit its use only to periods of 'profoundest peace'. Nevertheless it was the French fleet in the Mediterranean that was regarded as the greatest threat. The Admiralty felt that Black Sea operations were simply impossible unless the French had been neutralised, and called on the government to abandon the idea of defending Constantinople at all. Either that, or resistance to a Russian attack on the Straits would be 'across the ruins of the French fleet'. Later Salisbury concluded that 'our sailors, under the altered conditions of warfare, have no stomach for a hazardous attack [on the Bosphorus]', and predicted that Russia's possession of the Ottoman capital was a matter of time. Salisbury suggested an understanding with Russia in 1898, which allowed for the mutual recognition of spheres of influence in Persia, Turkey and China, which was eventually achieved in the Anglo-Russian Entente of 1907.

British naval supremacy was still evident in the 1890s

Yet despite the difficulties anticipated in future conflict, primarily caused by improvements to coastal defence and anti-shipping weapons like the torpedo and sea mine, it would be wrong to overemphasise British fears. There was a determination, part government-led and part popular, that Britain would retain its naval supremacy, and that its naval power would ensure the maintenance of the Empire. In 1897, at the Spithead review, there was an obvious satisfaction at the size and strength of the Royal Navy. There was also a recognition that Britain held some of the key strategic positions of the world, such as Gibraltar, Singapore, and the Cape. In 1899, British naval power enabled the army to deploy its largest ever concentration of forces, several thousand miles from the United Kingdom, and sustain them there throughout the South African War. The greatest difficulty was not in deciding the size and deployment of the Royal Navy, but in solving the problems of increasing costs and the means by which the Navy could be brought to bear against their continental adversaries in a period of rapid change.

The Naval Defence Act showed British determination to retain command of the seas

In March 1889, the Conservatives announced their intention to maintain the 'two power standard' whereby the Royal Navy would be maintained at twice the size of any two powers put together, and introduced the Naval Defence Act which entailed an expenditure of £21.5 million. Ten new battleships were to be constructed, as well as a sizeable flotilla of smaller vessels. Nevertheless, there were still demands to rectify Britain's naval weaknesses *vis-à-vis* the French in 1893. The debate in the press was as heated as in Parliament, and in early 1894 it was announced that seven new battleships would be built. This was the issue that Gladstone, still dedicated to the responsibility of retrenchment, could not agree to and he resigned a few days before the government's announcement.

Kennedy believes that British fears of rival fleets were exaggerated

According to Kennedy, there was a tendency to ignore the weaknesses of the Russian and French fleets and only to see faults in the Royal Navy. The Russian fleet was confined to training on land for long periods and they lacked skills in gunnery and navigation. The Russian fleets were slow, and classes of vessels were not mutually supporting. Ultimately these weaknesses were exposed at the battle of Tsushima (1905) in the Russo-Japanese war. Even a combination of Russian and French fleets would have been less damaging than the Navy League (a reform pressure group) argued. There was no experience of combined operations, language and signalling would have created difficulties in command and control, and even concentration in the Mediterranean could have been countered by a defensive posture around Gibraltar and Alexandria, with trade re-routed around the Cape. Kennedy concludes that the threat encouraged the Royal Navy to abandon its penny packeting of ships around the globe in favour of concentration in more powerful fleets.

Mahan's theories attributed Britain's success to the Royal Navy

A.J. Marder noted that interest in the Royal Navy was stimulated by a fear of foreign threats, and the exaggerated reports of naval enthusiasts. The most famous and influential theorist was the American, Alfred T. Mahan. His book, *The Influence of Sea Power Upon History 1660–1783* (1890), found a receptive audience in Britain. It was an attractive explanation for past imperial growth, but also a comforting prediction, in an age of increasing rivalry, that the possession of small island or coastal bases was infinitely preferable in strategic terms to large land masses. So too, was Mahan's belief that in future wars the naval blockade would prove an effective way of bringing an enemy to its knees. Mahan advocated the formation of large concentrated battlefleets as forces that would protect the most vital of all commercial activities – colonial trade.

Mahan's views coincided with a desire to expand the navy

It is tempting to attribute to Mahan the shaping of British naval strategy, with greater concentration of fleets and an emphasis on the 'Blue Water School' (spending on the navy rather than the army). In fact, Mahan's views coincided with a trend that was already evident. The 1888 Defence Committee had already placed more importance on the Royal Navy and it would be fairer to say that Mahan embodied what the public and navalists wanted to hear at exactly the right time. Kennedy argues that, in fact, the navalists were blinded by faith in Mahan's ideas to the true picture of Britain's relative naval decline. He states that the decline was the result of Britain's loss of industrial lead over America and other European powers, and a waning of sea power in relation to land power.

Paul Kennedy's views can be criticised

Although Eric Hobsbawm argued that this relative decline affected only industry and not finance or shipping, Kennedy believes that Britain failed to meet the maritime challenge too. A growing obsolescence in industry directly affected her naval development and competitiveness, whilst contributory factors, such a refusal to abandon free trade in the teeth of other powers' protectionism, and chronic complacency, accelerated the inevitable loss of paramountcy. However, efforts of imperial consolidation had been attempted long before Kennedy had acknowledged (the Imperial Conferences of 1887 and 1897, and the use of troops from the 'white dominions' were proof of that) whilst the inauguration of the

Defence Committees showed how seriously the British government took the naval threat, which refutes Kennedy's assertion that complacency reigned.

The principal concern for governments was the sheer cost of naval defence

Funding the Royal Navy was a major problem for governments in the last decades of the nineteenth century. Whereas a ninety-gun ship of the line in the 1850s cost in the region of £108,000, a screw propeller increased it to £151,000. Turbines, larger guns and iron-cladding or iron hulls meant a steady rise in expense. By 1893, when the *Majestic* was laid down, the cost per battleship was £1 million, and naval estimates rose from £11 million in 1883 to £18.7 million in 1896, reaching £34 million in 1903.

Foreign policy and the European powers: 'splendid isolation'

Splendid isolation referred to Britain's powerful world position

Salisbury realised that the key threats in the 1890s were France and Russia. They were imperial rivals and in secret they were allies. Instead of Britain forming alliances with other powers (which had been the response of Germany and Austria, and later, Italy), Salisbury preferred to reach bilateral agreements to settle specific problems. He did not want 'obligations and entanglements' which committed Britain to a war under different and unsuitable circumstances. Robert Taylor called this 'limited liability'. Its nickname, after the Canadian Prime Minister used it in 1896, was 'splendid isolation'. This implied that Britain was so powerful as to have no need of allies. Her navy and her Empire furnished her with the resources to withstand any attack. However, Salisbury only used the term with irony, suggesting that he was aware that isolation was recognised as a weakness. Historian John Charmley argues that 'splendid isolation' was a subtle game of staving off commitments to other European powers. Charmley believes Salisbury played this game with skill. This may be so, but it was essentially reactive; that is, Salisbury was responding to events and the initiatives of other powers. This may explain why Salisbury referred to his policy as 'putting out boathooks'.

Salisbury wanted to avoid imperial expansion

Salisbury was eager not to over-extend the Empire. He saw the need to secure the most vital parts of the world against other powers, but wanted to limit expansion. Exasperated, he once said of generals who urged the annexation of the Red Sea area, that they would insist on the 'defence of the Moon' to defend it 'from Mars'. However, Salisbury did support the extension of British control in East Africa and the Sudan in order to protect Egypt from French or German interference. This in turn secured the Eastern Mediterranean sea lanes and the route to India.

Is it valid to describe British policy as one of 'splendid isolation'?

Was there really a policy of splendid isolation? Although Britain had no formal alliances with other European Great Powers, it did have commitments of a limited nature. For example, Britain was the guarantor of Belgian neutrality ever since the country gained its independence in 1839. Gladstone prevented the invasion of Belgium in 1870 at the outbreak of the Franco-Prussian War, and Britain went to war in 1914 to defend Belgium against the German armies that had violated its neutrality. Belgium was therefore an important reason for Britain to participate in European affairs.

Britain had commitments to other countries in the Mediterranean

Britain protected Italian waters under the terms of the Mediterranean Agreement 1887, and through an 'exchange of notes' had friendly understandings with Spain and Austria-Hungary. Collectively, they agreed to preserve the *status quo* in the Mediterranean. However, although these notes carried no obligations, there would be an expectation that Britain would take some action if France or Russia tried to alter the balance of power in the region. On the Atlantic coast, an alliance with Portugal dating from the Napoleonic Wars in the early nineteenth century was still extant.

Britain had imperial commitments that could involve other European powers

Britain had protectorates over Afghanistan, the Sudan, Egypt, Bechuanaland and Uganda. There was a danger that other European powers could dispute Britain's influence. For example, Russia's interest in Afghanistan prompted a war between the Afghans and the British in 1878–80. Relations between Britain and Russia remained poor for decades. Britain's occupation of Egypt in 1882 angered France. French troops marched into and claimed the Sudan during the British reoccupation of the region in 1898.

Verdict on 'splendid isolation'

The historian C.A. Leeds described the splendid isolation as: 'A vague title without beginning or end'. Britain had no firm allies amongst the Great Powers when all the others, except the USA, did. The Franco-Russian Alliance had brought France and Russia together in 1894 whilst the Triple Alliance between Germany, Austria-Hungary and Italy (and later Romania) was concluded in 1883. Salisbury wanted to work with the old Concert of Europe, delicately balancing the two blocs but avoiding commitments to both. Chamberlain, by contrast, advocated a German alliance. This was never concluded because it appeared to the Germans to be directed against Russia. They were concerned that in the event of war, an alliance with Britain would mean they would bear the brunt of a continental war against Russia whilst Britain patrolled the seas. It was unsurprising that Germany looked to Austria as another continental power for assistance, not to the maritime British Empire. Britain was therefore isolated and was reliant on the supremacy of the Royal Navy and the land forces from the

United Kingdom and the Empire. Britain could regard this isolation as 'splendid' so long as her strength lasted. However, at the end of the century, Britain's maritime strength was challenged by European navies and the army suffered a series of setbacks in the South African War.

Foreign policy 1886–1899

Rebellion erupted in the Balkans between 1885 and 1886 threatening peace

Despite the creation of Serbia, Montenegro and Bulgaria in 1878, the Balkans of South-East Europe were dominated by the Ottoman Empire. Russia had assisted in the creation and liberation of Bulgaria during the Russo-Turkish War of 1877–78, but, in order to control the mouth of the Danube, Russian officials were influential in the Bulgarian government and Russian officers 'advised' the Bulgarian army. There seems little doubt that Bulgaria was regarded as a springboard to Constantinople and the strategically vital Straits. Control of the Straits would give the Russians a warm water access to southern Russia, thus avoiding the obstacle to commerce caused by the freezing of the Baltic. In 1885, the people of Eastern Roumelia, an Ottoman province adjacent to Bulgaria, rebelled and demanded union with their Bulgarian brothers. Salisbury's initial reaction was to oppose the Roumelians and back the Ottomans because he knew of the Russian influence in Bulgaria; any extension of Bulgaria was thus an extension of Russian rule in the Balkans. However, anti-Russian protests in Bulgaria itself seemed to indicate that far from being a Russian military staging post, Bulgaria might become a bulwark against Russia. As Disraeli's Foreign Secretary at the Congress of Berlin (1878), Salisbury had opposed a bigger Bulgaria, so he announced his switch to support of the anti-Russian Bulgaria with the phrase: 'We backed the wrong horse at Berlin'. The Russian threat had dictated Salisbury's views during the crisis, but for the first time the old defence policy of backing the Ottomans was redundant.

The scramble for Africa affected relations with other European powers

The extension of control by the British, French and German authorities in West Africa made a collision of interests likely, so an international conference was called by the German Chancellor Bismarck. It met in November 1884 and completed its tasks in February 1885. The conference was significant in that it laid down guidelines for the delimitation of European spheres of influence. The result was the rapid partition of the subcontinent, but also the avoidance of conflict between the European powers.

The Mediterranean Agreements, 1887, indicated Britain was 'splendidly isolated'

This was an example of 'limited liability'. There was no obligation on Britain, but Salisbury obtained the support of other European powers to preserve the *status quo* in the Mediterranean.

The Venezuela Dispute (1895) showed that Britain did not need allies
Chamberlain obtained support from other powers, including the USA, to uphold British claims to territory in South America against Venezuela.

There was ambiguity about Britain's isolated strength in the Eastern Mediterranean
When the Turks attacked Christian Armenians in 1896, massacring them, Salisbury wanted joint condemnation and action from the European Great Powers. Germany refused, as it was courting Turkish support for a railway project (which would eventually dominate the region). The Russians feared supporting Armenian rebels against legitimate authority because it might encourage similiar problems inside Russia. Britain was alone in its condemnation. In the Greco-Turkish War (1897–98), however, the Royal Navy assisted the Greeks who had been repulsed from Crete and had lost part of Thessaly. Crete was given back to the Greeks. The power of the Royal Navy reinforced her status of 'splendid isolation'.

Britain followed her own policy in the Far East
The Japanese treaty with China after the Sino-Japanese War of 1894–95 (the Treaty of Shimonsekei) was condemned by all the European powers, except Britain. Rosebery's Liberal government didn't feel it could protest in case it damaged British trading interests in the region. By 1898, China appeared to be on the verge of collapse. The Russians forced the Chinese to let them build a railway across Manchuria and later, after the Boxer Rebellion (1900), they took Mongolia to 'restore order'. They also took up possession of Port Arthur, a strategic port on the Yellow Sea. The Germans took Kiaochow by way of 'compensation' for their rival's annexation. Britain's policy had always been the 'open door'; all should be allowed to trade freely and no single power should gain possession of Chinese territory, although Britain herself had a lease on Hong Kong. However, the seizure of ports and lands by Japan, Russia and Germany demonstrated that Britain had to act to preserve its interests. It did so by taking a lease on Wei Hei Wei in 1898. However, the rivalry of the powers should not be exaggerated. During the Boxer Rebellion, the European powers did co-operate (a joint military force made its way to Beijing under British command), so alliances were perhaps unnecessary in colonial issues where they all shared a common purpose.

Britain still had a formidable military arsenal
The reconquest of the Sudan (1896–98) and the South African War (1899–1902), even the Pathan Rising on the North-West Frontier of India (1897–98) had been major military operations but there had been no need for European allies. The colonies sent troops and supplies and the Empire appeared to be a powerful bloc.

Britain was prepared to threaten force against France
The Fashoda Incident (1898), when a small French force claimed the southern Sudan at the same time as the British, showed how powerful Britain was. The Royal Navy could prevent any French operation across the Mediterranean or the

English Channel. The Russian fleet were too far away to help, and uninterested in the French African Empire. The French felt that any large-scale troop deployment against Britain would leave her exposed to attack by Germany. Salisbury was able to obtain a French climb-down, but he was eager to assuage any feeling of humiliation which might provoke a desire for revenge

Was there an alternative to 'splendid isolation'?

Britain was clearly a powerful military and naval power with an Empire that offered troops and supplies. The British Empire was also dangerously dispersed across the globe which demanded a military or naval presence everywhere. Rosebery felt that Britain needed to avoid conflict or else be engaged in 'forty wars at any one time'. Salisbury pursued the only truly viable policy of trying to avoid commitments, whilst maintaining good relations with all the Great Powers. However, the ambitions of Russia, France and Germany meant that threats had to be met by maintaining a strong global position and international prestige.

The British Empire and new imperialism

The controversy of new imperialism

Britain's Empire expanded dramatically in the last quarter of the nineteenth century, with new colonies added in Africa and Asia. Historians disagree on the motives for imperialism, and even find it difficult to reach a consensus about the nature of imperialism. Britain's imperial expansion was so rapid, in fact, that most of the contemporary explanations of it came after the event, which seems to indicate that the Victorians were trying to make sense of what had happened instead of developing some new ideology that they wished to fulfil. Nevertheless, Britain was already a vast imperial power before the nineteenth century, and its existing colonies exerted a considerable influence on its development.

Britain's Empire dated back to the 1490s

The paradox about explanations for imperialism was that it was not new at all. As early as the fifteenth century, traders and explorers had made their way around the globe and established coastal trading posts. Small colonies of settlers, such the Spanish settlements in the Americas, were usually engaged in the exploitation of resources, the most famous being gold and silver. The British experiments in the early seventeenth century were not always a great success, and their chief rivals were the Dutch, Spanish, and later, the French. However, they were very successful in driving out these rivals in the eighteenth century and established colonies and outposts in North America, the East and West Indies, the Pacific Islands and in India. The means that enabled the British to do this was a powerful navy and its merchant fleet. However, Britain was seriously checked in its imperial aspirations by the American War of Independence (1775–83) and began to look more carefully at the development of its eastern possessions.

Nineteenth century imperialism built on its existing trade system

British imperial expansion in the nineteenth century can be divided into two phases. The first involved the same sort of development as previous centuries with trading posts being established on the coasts of China and Africa. New sources of raw materials and markets continued to be the motive for the development of trade. At times, that trade required military protection. Some new developments included the acquisition of Cape Colony in 1815, but it was the need to secure revenues and existing possessions that led to the wholesale annexation of territories in the Indian subcontinent. Older empires were subjected either to British military action to open up trading agreements (China) or compelled to sign defensive treaties (Persia). Britain fought a series of expensive wars to ensure the security of its possessions, including campaigns in Abyssinia (1868), the Crimea (1854–56) and Afghanistan (1838–42). The East India Company (a private business with its own army and bureaucracy under British government supervision), was abolished and replaced by the direct rule of the British government in 1858 after the Indian Mutiny (1857–58).

The second phase of expansion was called 'new imperialism'

In a speech in 1872, Disraeli redefined imperialism, not as a simple trading activity, but as a mutually beneficial relationship. Britain would, as a duty, bring the benefits of civilisation to 'primitive' peoples. These were 'courage, discipline, patience, reverence for public law, and respect for national rights'. In return, Britain would enjoy the fruits of the Empire in the form of wealth and prestige. There was an implicit call for British men and women to go abroad in a spirit of self-sacrifice, enduring tropical heat, diseases, and hostile native peoples. Kipling, the writer and poet, later described this as 'The white man's burden'. Disraeli also hoped that colonial peoples would form a bond with Britain and they would mutually support each other economically and militarily. However, Disraeli had been disapproving of aggressive wars in the name of imperialism and, ironically, it was Gladstone's invasion of Egypt which appeared to spark a scramble for territory by the European powers (although the French invasion of Tunisia in 1881 could also be seen as responsible for this).

Historians have identified economic motives for imperial expansion

It could be argued that the industrial revolution in Britain stimulated a huge demand for raw materials, some of which were not available in Britain. In addition, the scale of production was such that Britain was able to manufacture goods more cheaply and more quickly than traditional economies that relied on handmade products. This suggests that the search for raw materials, and markets for finished goods, acted as a spur to imperialism. However, J. Hargreaves, C. Newbury and D. Fieldhouse have argued that imperialism really developed from a desire to protect Britain's trade. In other words, territorial annexation occurred when trade sources, routes or markets were in danger. Therefore, it was easy for Disraeli to advocate expansion when British traders felt threatened by the commerce of other European powers in the 1870s. Britain's leadership of new imperialism can be explained by the existence of the older imperial possessions: they were able to convert their coastal possessions, acquired long before, into colonies that stretched into the interior. When the British did this, other Europeans did the same.

There were problems with the economic theory of expansion

An examination of British trade and investment revealed that Britain did not always acquire territory to protect its most valuable regions of commerce. For example, the South American states were valuable trading partners but they were not part of Britain's Empire. In 1953, R. Robinson and J. Gallagher argued that the British really preferred to have 'informal control', that is, economic influence without the expense of political control. Government offices, military forces, civil servants, public services and administration had to be provided in the colonies, but informal spheres of influence were 'empire on the cheap'. This is sometimes referred to as 'reluctant imperialism'. In 1961, they developed their theory and argued that the event which had initiated the 'scramble for Africa' was the invasion of Egypt in 1882. The primary motive for this had been the desire to protect British trade routes when informal influence broke down. In West Africa, they stated that African resistance had encouraged the British to annex more territory, but again, they did so 'reluctantly'. Robinson and Gallagher concluded that it was at the periphery, rather than at government level, that one would find the motive for annexation.

Imperialism was thought to be a form of capitalism

J.A. Hobson's *Imperialism: A Study* (1902) was really an explanation for the outbreak of the Anglo-Boer War (1899–1902) which he blamed on the capitalist 'Randlords' in Britain and Johannesburg. He tried to argue that the war had been fought because the British sought to acquire gold in the Transvaal. He developed his ideas by tying in the division of rich and poor in Britain. Because the poor couldn't buy enough of what the capitalists could produce at home, he argued, the capitalists sought to invest their 'surplus' capital overseas. The Bolshevik leader V.I. Lenin felt that overseas investment and the subsequent acquisition of colonies was an inevitable stage of capitalism. He stated that imperialism could therefore only be understood by studying the economies of Europe. To Lenin 'Imperialism is monopoly capitalism'. These theories therefore put the emphasis on processes beyond the decisions of governments. However, the flaw in these theories was that neither explained imperialism in anything other than economic terms.

P.J. Cain and A.G. Hopkins revived the economic explanation

Cain and Hopkins argued that a depression in British manufacturing was the incentive to secure guaranteed markets and sources of raw materials. They stated that increasing foreign competition in traditional European and American markets drove British businesses towards the colonies and developing world. In particular, they point to the growth of financial institutions in the City of London and the close connection these developed with the imperial government. They labelled these élites the 'gentlemen capitalists' and argued that landed aristocrats and financiers in the City co-operated to invest surplus capital with a return some time in the future. Cain and Hopkins therefore link the continued domination of financiers and aristocrats in the British economy, the collaboration of men drawn from wealthy classes in the South-East of England, with the extension of the British Empire.

Individuals played a part in extending British rule

There was a nineteenth century school of historical thought that argued that history should be studied through 'great men' (and women too, but the Victorians placed the emphasis on their male leaders). Exceptional individuals certainly played a part in the expansion of British rule in Africa. Cecil Rhodes would fall into this category. His companies developed diamond mining at Kimberley in British Cape Colony and gold mining on the Witwatersrand in the Transvaal which attracted interest from the British government. He advocated the annexation of Bechuanaland, independently annexed a massive territory called Rhodesia, and conspired to topple the Transvaal government in 1895 in favour of British rule. Rhodes also aimed to see the construction of a railway from Cape Town to Cairo which would dominate the trade of Africa. Although no railway was built, Rhodes was an inspiration to other imperialists. However, some of the missionaries and explorers, such as David Livingstone or Henry Morton Stanley also advertised the potential of Africa. They paved the way for later claims to British territories such as Kenya and Uganda.

Military imperialism was also a factor in the expansion of the British Empire

The British army was engaged in a series of 'small wars' throughout the nineteenth century. Bruce Vandervort has explained the partition of Africa as a process led by European forces. The actions of Admiral Seymour and General Wolseley were important to the occupation of Egypt in 1882. General Kitchener reconquered the Sudan in 1898. Zululand and the Boer Republics were also absorbed after British military action.

Post-colonial historians have referred to an ideological motive for imperialism

Post-colonial theorists argue that there was a strong, if subtle, imperialist ideology in Britain. They argue that a collection of supremacist values coincided with an economic, naval and military superiority in the early nineteenth century. These values included patriotism and the desire to maintain the status of being a Great Power. Careful analysis of the 'sub texts' in historical documents, it is argued, reveal the belief system of the period. Disraeli had once argued that Empire would make Britain a cosmopolitan country and a world power, but Liberal critics like Gladstone thought that further expansion was immoral unless it could be demonstrated how benefits might be bestowed on the subject peoples. The Liberal criticism of the South African War also suggests that the ideology was not unbridled. Indeed, the chief criticism of the post-colonialists is that they select the texts for interpretation too narrowly, or label all texts, and therefore all historical figures, as 'unreliable' or 'fictional'. The problem is that they fail to appreciate a different value system from a bygone era sufficiently. Cain and Hopkins argue that the Empire offered a way to combat democratic and republican impulses and a way to preserve the privileges of the gentlemen-élites. But this puts the cart before the horse; the formulation of ideologies actually followed the process of imperialism, they did not lead it.

The search for explanations of expansion conceals British 'reluctance'
Unfortunately, the desire to find the motive for expansion can obscure the fact that British governments were usually reluctant to extend British rule. Investment was concentrated in regions with secure futures, rather than undeveloped or unstable tribal states or colonies. Britain's volume of trade and investment with the USA and Argentina was considerable: for example, 25% of all British investment in 1913 was with Latin America. Bernard Porter argues that the commercial aspect was only one part of Britain's influence and described the formal Empire as 'merely the surface outcrops of a much broader geological reef'. Moreover, it was necessary to avoid conflict so as not to damage the finances of the City of London. This was vital, argue Cain and Hopkins, because British manufacturing was in decline and finance was progressing. Annexations were dictated by the desire to protect property, credit and the flow of trade. If credit was more important, it was therefore vital that Britain avoided unnecessary wars. Intervention would therefore take place with considerable reluctance.

Military factors could also deter expansion
Mountainous frontiers which were easy to defend, such as the Hindu Kush and Himalayas, made further expansion northwards from India unnecessary. Equally, it should be noted that military annexation was expensive. There had been a public enquiry because the Abyssinia campaign of 1868 had cost so much money. There was also a risk of conflict with other European powers or the possibility of defeat at the hands of colonial enemies with a consequent loss of prestige. In 1881, British forces had been surprised and defeated at Majuba Hill by rebellious Transvaal Boers. The Italians did worse. They were defeated by Abyssinian warriors at Adowa in 1896, prompting the Italian liberal government to abandon expansion in Africa altogether. Britain had no wish to suffer a similar humiliation.

Sovereignty prevented the partition of China and the Ottoman Empire
There was a reluctance to annex complete sovereign states such as the Ottoman or Chinese Empires which the British regarded as old civilisations. However, the interest of other European powers also acted as a brake to partition. This did not apply to black states such as Zululand, or the Kingdom of the Matabele. Consequently, it could be argued that Great Power rivalry could determine whether a territory was annexed or not.

Verdict on new imperialism: no single factor can explain it
David Fieldhouse was arguably the most accurate when he called for historians to weigh up each episode of imperial expansion on its own merits. On balance, it would be most convincing to argue that the partition of Africa was a process which combined many of the factors listed above. There was no monocausal explanation, and there would be a changing relative importance in each factor depending on local circumstances.

The scramble for Africa: West and East Africa

In West Africa, older colonies were extended inland. Primarily, this was driven by the desire for greater security for traders and missionaries against indigenous peoples, or other powers. Gambia and Sierra Leone were extended, whilst the Gold Coast was enlarged following a military campaign against 'King Coffee' of the Ashanti (Asante) in 1873–74. Britain had annexed Lagos in 1861, but the Royal Niger Company (chartered in 1886) acquired more territory deep into the interior. Nevertheless, the prevalence of malaria prevented large-scale, permanent occupation for many years. In East Africa, British Somalialand was seized in order to protect the trade routes in the Red Sea and Indian Ocean. The British East Africa Company (1888) drove forward and annexed the area named Kenya, whilst a protectorate was established over Uganda, the source of the Nile. Although apparently fantastic now, there was a concern in the 1890s that the Nile could be redirected, thus destroying Egypt's economy and destabilising British control of the Eastern Mediterranean. The reconquest of the Sudan in 1898 ensured British control of the whole length of the Nile. Once this artery of Africa was secured, Cecil Rhodes proposed a railway should be constructed that would run from the Cape to Cairo, drawing trade from every province of Africa. Typically grandiose and ambitious, the railway was never completed although an air service was established in the 1930s.

British rule in Asia

Britain's rule in Asia was already well established
Although the scramble for Africa provides a dramatic example of new imperialism, it should be noted that Asia was also the scene of intense rivalry and rapid annexation. Once again, Britain's imperial expansion emerged from older possessions. British control in India dated back to the eighteenth century, part of the Malay Peninsula had been British from 1798, Singapore's naval base had been constructed in 1819 and British trading relationships in South and South-East Asia had been established in the seventeenth century. However, there were new additions after 1870. In 1877 and 1888, Britain obtained North Borneo and Sarawak, and Papua was taken in 1884. Britain annexed Upper Burma in 1886 partly in response to the French annexation of Indo-China in 1884.

Late nineteenth century
Aim: Uphold British interests
▶ Defend United Kingdom and the British Empire possessions against invasion
▶ Protect British trade
▶ Preserve peace and therefore the circulation of world trade

Main threats:
France and Russia

Significant flashpoints:
The Nile (French threat to control of headwaters) – led to Fashoda Incident, 1898.
Afghanistan (Russian threat to India) – led to the Penjdeh Incident, 1885.
The Mediterranean (naval threats to British trade routes) – led to the occupation of Egypt, 1882.
Africa and Asia (other powers) – led to a 'scramble' for territory to acquire resources in the future.

Settlements:
British governments sought to avoid pacts or alliances that might commit them to war in the future, but Mediterranean Agreeements at least preserved the *status quo*.

Early twentieth century
Aim: Unchanged

Main threats:
Germany
Some internal unrest in the Empire

Significant flashpoints:
The world's oceans (German naval threat) – led to disputes in North Africa and Turkey, 1905–1913.
Asia and Africa (Germany acquired territory there but wanted more) – Germany supplied arms to the Boers of southern Africa in 1890s.
South Africa (Boers clash with Britain's hegemonic status) – led to the South African War, 1899–1902.
Ireland (Irish Nationalists demanded self-rule) – led to a potential civil war in 1912–14.

Settlements:
Settled differences with France and Rusia and concentrated on the potential German threat.

Fig. 4. Foreign policy: aims and priorities.

There was a threat to the borders of India

The Second Afghan War (1878–80) proved that the British were determined to make Afghanistan part of their sphere of influence and thus protect the North-Western approaches to India. Nevertheless, the Russians also knew this might be played to their advantage. Threats towards the Indian frontier could clearly distract British attentions from the Eastern Mediterranean. Many people in India remained convinced that the Russian annexations in Central Asia were only the prelude to an attack on the Indian frontier. The extent of Russian acquisitions was certainly considerable. Between 1873 and 1895 the gap between the two Empires shrunk from 2000 miles to 20 miles. It was the relentless, creeping nature of this expansion which the British in India found so disconcerting. The Liberal Party considered this threat to be nothing more than a 'chimera' (as John Bright had remarked). They supported Gladstone's belief that direct negotiation with the Russians was the only policy to adopt. Yet many small oases and cities fell to the Russian army including Bokhara, Tashkent, Samarkand and Khiva. In March 1885, Russian troops attacked the Afghans at Penjdeh. Gladstone, and then Salisbury, negotiated a settlement to avert a conflict, but there were subsequent war scares.

The North-West Frontier was the scene of frequent conflict

The British had to hold down a population who resented British rule in a series of campaigns on the North-West Frontier, the largest of which took place in 1897. Afghanistan, although allied to Britain, intrigued against British rule amongst the frontier tribes. British 'agents' established close personal relations with tribesmen and attempts were made to recruit the hill fighters into British units. However, banditry and resistance to British influence continued throughout the period.

The British Raj in India was a source of pride to the British

In 1877, the Imperial Assemblage of Dehli was a carefully stage-managed *puja* (ceremony) designed to confirm the relationship of the British with their Indian subjects. The Queen was created Empress of India, elevating her position to that of successor to the Mughal emperors. It was thought that the Raj relied on the collaboration of the Indian Princes who were influential with the people. As a result, they were patronised like feudal knights: protected by the monarchy in return for loyal service. Nevertheless, British rule also relied on the acquiescence of the people which could only be maintained through efficient administration (carried out by the Indian Civil Service) and effective public works. Although considerable effort was made to develop the Punjab with irrigation, and the rest of India with investment, famine relief and railways, the creation of the Indian National Congress in 1885 heralded the start of a long struggle for independence. However, this should not be exaggerated. India remained loyal and provided the largest single source of manpower for imperial forces anywhere in the British Empire. Congress remained, according to Lord Dufferin, a 'microscopic minority' who were eager to profess their loyalty to the British crown. Despite riots against anti-plague regulations in the 1890s, India remained at peace until the Bengal partition controversy in 1905.

Britain's primary interest in China was trade

Two wars had been fought (1839–42 and 1858–60) to prise open Chinese trade and Britain had established 'free trade' ports, the most important of which were Shanghai, Canton and Hong Kong. However, Russia, Germany and Japan all sought to obtain greater influence over China. 'Spheres of influence' were established; informal orbits of exclusive control. A carve-up of China seemed to be imminent. Japan defeated the Chinese in 1895 and forced Peking to make concessions, but this prompted Germany to annex Kiaochow and Russia to seize Port Arthur. Salisbury did not feel that Britain was strong enough to protect the entire Chinese coastline and he was pessimistic about British influence in the Far East. In 1898, Britain leased Wei Hei Wei for 99 years, but there seemed to be no answer to Britain's predicament. However, the Great Powers co-operated in the defeat of a Chinese rebellion in 1900 and Lord Lansdowne concluded the Anglo-Japanese Alliance in 1902. The alliance is seen by some as the end of isolation, but in fact it may have confirmed it. Britain had no European allies and saw the 1902 alliance as a marriage of convenience.

The dominions

Australia experienced rapid development in the late nineteenth century

Wool and wheat were two of Australia's largest exports, despite droughts and falling prices in the 1890s. Meat was exported with the development of refrigeration in the 1880s and gold mining continued to attract investment. Australia itself was divided. Each state had its own tariff regulations, and, with the exception of the Northern Territory, was self-governing. However, German annexations (Samoa and New Guinea) in 1899 and Japanese immigration led to talks on union. In 1900, the Commonwealth of Australia Act established a federated nation whereby each state retained a parliament, but all acknowledged that Canberra's assembly was the primary decision-making body for national issues or foreign policy. In 1905, the 'white Australia' policy restricted the numbers of Japanese and Asian immigrants entering the country, but the influx of British continued so that, by 1914, there were five million 'Australians'.

New Zealand had a progressive outlook

The bitter legacy of the New Zealand Wars (1846–47, 1857–69) was the expropriation of land from the Maoris by white settlers, and a decline in the Maori population. However, by the 1890s, the Maori population was recovering, and land disputes had been largely settled when Maoris were given full and equal rights. Economically, meat and butter exports were considerable, dwarfing its gold and mineral reserves. However, New Zealand was remarkable for its degree of state ownership and universal suffrage. From the outset, the colony had been reliant on central direction, rather than private enterprise, for its railways, banks, schools and telegraph. By 1900, the state was responsible for the construction of hospitals and loans to build workers' houses. New Zealand's government also implemented old age pensions, labour exchanges and compensation for employee's injuries in the workplace. All men were given the vote in 1889, and all women in 1893. These reforms were several decades ahead of Britain itself.

Canada's history in the nineteenth century was one of gradual consolidation

Four provinces had united under the British North America Act in 1867, and, in 1870, the Hudson's Bay Company territories joined, from which Manitoba was created. In 1871, British Columbia agreed to join if a railway was constructed to link it to the east coast. The vast Canadian Pacific Railway was completed in 1885 and it made possible the exploitation of the prairies. Progress into this area had been slow because of hostile natives, and military operations had culminated in the suppression of the Louis Riel rebellion in 1885. After that date, the population rapidly increased, Alberta and Saskatchewan were formed (1905), and, by 1914, the wheat crop had increased twenty times. Emigration from Britain continued throughout the period too. All these factors leave a question mark over the Canadian 'identity' before the First World War. Newfoundland, the oldest colony, refused to join the rest of Canada before the war, and each state retained an attitude of 'frontier independence'. In Britain, there was considerable criticism of Sir John Macdonald's government when it introduced protectionism in 1878, whilst the Canadians were uninterested in Chamberlain's ideas of imperial preference. Canadian loyalty to the Empire was tested by the First World War, but many of the 'Canadian' soldiers who served in the war were often recent emigrants from Britain.

The South African War, 1899–1902

Causes of the South African War

Hopes for the confederation of Southern Africa had experienced a setback when the Transvaal broke free of British rule in 1881. However, it was felt that the two Boer Republics, Transvaal and Orange Free State, were agricultural backwaters and no threat to British control of the Cape. In the northern Cape, diamond mining added to the mineral wealth, and economic supremacy of the British colony. In 1885, Britain annexed southern Bechuanaland in response to the German seizure of German South West Africa (1884). In 1889, the British South Africa Company, under the ambitious Cecil Rhodes, took vast swathes of territory to the north of Transvaal and named it Rhodesia. However, Rhodes did not find the minerals he was looking for in order to extend his company fortunes. Instead, gold was discovered on the Witwatersrand, later Johannesburg, in the Transvaal in 1886. Although Rhodes was able to acquire some share of the Rand mining, he was one of several mine magnates who were frustrated by the government of Transvaal under President Paul Kruger. Kruger, like many of his countrymen, disliked the capitalists on the Rand. They resented the endless search for profit, preferring the guidance of Calvinist doctrine and the life of agriculturists. Kruger also recognised that the influx of miners, primarily from Britain and the Cape, was growing so fast that they threatened to outnumber the Boers. As a result, Kruger imposed punitive taxes on the mine owners and denied the *uitlanders* (outsiders) any political rights.

The British government was concerned about the shift of power to the Transvaal
Although gold was being sold on the world market, the Transvaal government's taxation gave the Boers a significant increase in national revenue. There was concern that, should the Boers continue to develop their country, they might replace the Cape's economic supremacy and with it, control of the whole of southern Africa. This concern was shared by Cecil Rhodes. Rhodes was eager to remove the burden of Kruger's government on Rand mining. He planned a rebellion by *uitlanders* to overthrow the Boers. Although arms had been smuggled into the Transvaal, the *coup* would be initiated by a mounted column under his Rhodesian colleague, Dr Leander Jameson. Rhodes secretly negotiated with the Colonial Secretary, Joseph Chamberlain, in order to launch the raid from British territory.

The Jameson Raid soured Anglo-Transvaal relations
In 1895, the raiders set off. Rhodes appeared to have been warned that the *uitlanders* had changed their mind about the planned rising, but he was too late to recall Jameson. The raiders were ambushed by Boer commandos and captured. Kruger agreed to hand over Jameson and his colleagues for trial in Britain, because they had broken international law, but he viewed the Rhodes' conspiracy as part of a British plan to annex the Transvaal. Rhodes resigned from the premiership of the Cape but Chamberlain was exonerated by a committee of enquiry. Kruger's response was to arm the Transvaal with modern weapons, particularly from Germany. The new High Commissioner to the Cape in 1897, Sir Alfred Milner, viewed the Transvaal's military expansion as further evidence that, unless action was taken by the British Empire, the Transvaal would dominate the region. Milner's plan was to see the Transvaal subordinated to British rule, and the Cape parliament dominated by British representatives. This would involve the removal of Kruger's régime and the federation of southern Africa. Milner also hoped that, like Canada, British settlers could be attracted to the region.

The outbreak of war was caused by a break down in the negotiations
In 1899, the murder of a *uitlander* by a Boer policeman on the Rand led to a petition from the foreign community for British protection. In May, Milner met Kruger at Bloemfontein to request that *uitlanders* be given the vote. Kruger knew that this would mean the swamping of the *Volkraad* (parliament) with British representatives and he refused. Kruger also refused to make any reductions in the punitive taxation of the mining operations, so it could be argued that he had some responsibility for the continuing antagonism between the Transvaal and the British. However, historian Iain Smith has shown how Milner engineered a war by making impossible demands on Kruger. Milner also ignored the peaceful

overtures of the moderate Boers (Jan Smuts and Louis Botha), and even misled Chamberlain by despatching inflammatory Boer responses by telegraph to London and more moderate Boer replies by slow steamer. Thomas Pakenham believes the greatest Boer mistake was to issue an ultimatum to the British in October 1899. This played into Milner's hands because he could argue that the British Empire had been challenged. With public opinion in the Cape and Britain united against Boer intransigence and aggression, war broke out. The Orange Free State joined the Transvaal in its offensive.

After initial Boer successes, the war swung in Britain's favour

The Boer war plan was to drive the British back to the coast of the Cape and force them to accept terms as they had in 1881. Initially, they outnumbered the British forces in South Africa and they quickly besieged the towns of Mafeking, Kimberley and Ladysmith. Using fieldcraft tactics and marksmanship perfected by hunting, the Boers defeated British troops who were more used to engaging tribal enemies who fought in the open. In December 1899, the British were checked three times in one 'Black Week' at Colenso, Stormberg and Magersfontein. However, the Boers lost the initiative by continuing the sieges. British reinforcements arrived led Lord Roberts, a soldier of considerable experience of war in South Asia. Whilst General Buller launched new attacks from Natal towards Ladysmith, Roberts defeated Boer forces at Paardeberg and then went on the capture Bloemfontein and Pretoria. Kruger fled to Holland and the war appeared to have been won.

To avoid defeat, the Boers turned to guerilla tactics

Even before Roberts had left South Africa, the Boers formed themselves into small units to raid British supply columns and attack railways. These guerilla forces outpaced the slow-moving British columns sent to intercept them. Lord Kitchener was tasked with bringing the guerilla war to an end. He divided the veld into huge zones, surrounded by barbed wire and blockhouses. These restricted the movements of the Boer commandos. British troops then formed huge lines which scoured the zones for pockets of resistance. These 'drives', which resembled a line of beaters for a shooting party, failed to capture the most notorious leaders, Smuts, de Wet and Botha. Kitchener, under political pressure to produce a victory, turned to a scorched earth policy to deprive the commandos of supplies. Women and children were herded into camps where many died from insanitary conditions or disease. Livestock was slaughtered and crops destroyed. Despite the criticism in Britain, especially from David Lloyd George, the tactics began to have an effect. In May 1902, with the Boers themselves divided over continuation of the war, the last of the 'bitter enders' gave up and signed a peace treaty at Vereiniging.

The outcome of the South African War was mixed for Britain

Opponents of the war were a minority labelled 'pro-Boers' and the election fought in 1900 was nick-named the 'khaki election' because it produced a massive

Conservative landslide. However, there was considerable criticism of the 'methods of barbarism' used by Kitchener to win the second phase of the war. Emily Hobhouse went out to South Africa to see for herself the conditions which prevailed in the civilian concentration camps. This was not the only controversy. Foreign powers saw the war as an example of Britain's greed and aggressiveness towards small nations. Some Liberals suspected that the war had been fought for gold and for the interests of a few capitalists. These factors combined to motivate the Boers, after the war, to see the struggle against Britain as the crucible of Afrikanerdom. Forged by their shared hardship, the Het Volk party won overwhelming support in the Cape parliament. Although Transvaal and Orange River Colony (as it was renamed) were incorporated in a self-governing federation (1907) and then a united country (1910), Milner's objectives were not really fulfilled. South Africa was Boer dominated, rather than ethnically British. The war had also been far more expensive than originally envisaged. Three million pounds was spent on the reconstruction of Boer farms and livestock, but the war itself had cost £222 million. To safeguard the future of South Africa within the Empire, the British government was keen to repair the damage done to relations between the Boers and the British, and they saw their peace terms and reconstruction as a 'magnanimous gesture'.

The significance of the South African War

The South African War left an important legacy, not just for Afrikaners, but also for Britain. It was the largest of the colonial wars and was one of the most difficult guerilla operations that the British army had fought in the nineteenth century; it was perhaps a foretaste of the decolonisation conflicts of the twentieth. It revealed serious deficiencies in the British army. Military reforms followed but there was a strong sense of wanting greater 'national efficiency' in Britain's defence and also in her political administration. Kipling wrote that Britain had had 'no end of a lesson'. Sadly, only in recent years has the full impact on the black population of South Africa emerged. Despite the contemporary view that this was a 'white man's war', black people were employed by both sides and even formed armed units. During the siege of Mafeking, it appears that thousands of black inhabitants died. There were also black concentration camps. After the war, the 1905 Native Affairs Commission recommended that reservations be set aside for black people largely on the American model. It was this segregation which ultimately developed into a discriminatory system against blacks.

Conclusions: the Empire is still an area of controversy

The British Empire still provokes intense historical debate. Yet there are broad conclusions which can be drawn about Britain's relations with other countries in this period. The mid-century optimism about trade and naval supremacy was threatened. Liberals continued to see the development of European economies as ultimately beneficial, reinforcing the effects of free trade. Conservatives and many manufacturers began to see other European powers as a threat. The foreign policies of both parties were marked by caution and although Britain did acquire vast new territories, this process was often without direct government support, or at least tempered by anxiety about over-reaching its resources. Salisbury exemplified that pessimism, and much of his intervention seemed motivated by a desire to secure what Britain already possessed. Popular attitudes towards the Empire reached a peak of enthusiasm in the 1890s. This may have provided a useful vehicle for the Conservatives to gather support, since they portrayed themselves as the party of the Empire. However, there was a darker side to this. Despite the British drive to eradicate slavery, a mission which dominated the nineteenth century, old prejudices based on cultural differences ossified into racial stereotyping. Given the European superiority in technology and the existence of global empires, this process is easier to understand even if difficult to empathise with. The South African War demonstrated that, against a well-armed opponent, Britain would be hard pressed. In 1902, the Japanese alliance may have ended isolation, or merely confirmed it, but the subsequent and urgent search to end points of conflict with its old enemies France and Russia confirmed that isolationism was limited.

Tutorial

Progress questions
1. Summarise the reasons why Britain acquired colonies in Africa between 1885 and 1902.

2. Why was Joseph Chamberlain a key figure in British imperial policy between 1895–1902? (Concentrate on his aims, his reforms, and his significance.)

3. Why was there tension in Southern Africa between the Boers and the British between 1838 and 1896?

4. How important was Cecil Rhodes to the extension of British rule in southern Africa?

5. Why did a war break out between the British and the Boers in 1899? Why do historians disagree about this?

Seminar discussion
1. Imperialism
a. Were all the examples of imperial expansion economically motivated?

b. Were individuals or processes more important, in other words was it premeditated by a few individuals, or an accidental outcome?

2. Britain's 'splendid isolation'
a. Were the British justified in their confidence of their isolation?

b. Did Salisbury's approach to dealing with the other European powers make any difference to their relations with Britain?

c. Was Great Power rivalry to blame for the partition of Africa, and Britain's other imperial annexations?

Practical assignment
1. Was Britain 'isolated' in the 1890s? List the ways in which this was an advantage, and the ways in which this was a disadvantage.

2. What incidents demonstrate Britain's 'splendid isolation' between 1895–1902? Make a list of events and annotate onto them an evaluation.

Study tips
1. Test yourself on the motives for the imperial expansion. Try to recall the main features of Britain's isolationist period. You need to be able to show both sides of an argument on these issues, rather than just listing the events. Can you show, for example, the extent to which the Anglo-Japanese Alliance (1902) was the end of isolation?

2. Note how France and Russia were Britain's rivals for most of the nineteenth century. In the early twentieth century that was to change dramatically when Britain settled its differences with France and Russia, but became concerned by German aggressiveness around the globe.

3. Be sure to differentiate between alliances and ententes. Be aware of what made Britain's isolation possible, such as its vast resources, and its army and navy.

4. By the end of this chapter you should be able to:
    ▶ explain why Africa was partitioned between 1884 and 1914
    ▶ explain why Britain was isolated between 1885 and 1902
    ▶ explain the deterioration of Anglo-German relations between 1900 and 1914
    ▶ identify 'British interests' in foreign and imperial policy.

6

New Liberalism, 1895–1914

One-minute summary – Although hopelessly divided over Ireland and out of office for most of the late nineteenth century, the Liberals swept back to power in 1906 in a landslide election victory. This puzzling result has appeared all the more curious because after 1906, the Liberals appeared to go into a long decline, culminating in a party split in 1916. After the war, the Liberals were effectively replaced as the main opposition to the Conservatives by Labour. Despite the decay, the Liberals passed a variety of far-reaching measures and probably laid the foundation of the welfare state. Their philosophy, New Liberalism, was motivated in part by a desire to tackle the problem of poverty, but the passion behind the ideas was provided by the inflammatory Lloyd George and the young Winston Churchill.

In this chapter you will learn:

▶ why the Conservatives were so heavily defeated in the 1905 election
▶ what New Liberalism was, and why it was regarded as necessary
▶ the ways in which it was new, and the extent to which it was different from Old Liberalism
▶ how far New Liberalism offered a real alternative to the electorate, or a solution to the rise of Labour.

The Conservatives and the 1905 election

The election of December 1905 was the biggest landslide ever to that date. There has been much speculation as to why the Conservative Party, that had dominated politics for so long, was defeated so roundly and why the Liberal Party, that seemed to be in terminal decline, won so convincingly. Was it the result of Conservative errors? L.C.B. Seaman called the election: 'An unjust verdict on Balfour's ministry'. Alternatively, it could be said that: 'Oppositions don't win elections, governments lose them'. In other words, the Liberals didn't really offer much that attracted the electorate, but the Conservatives alienated popular support in the years between 1900 (the year of the 'khaki election') and 1905. There may have been a series of factors which influenced the final outcome.

Ireland was no longer high on the political agenda
Despite the violence of earlier decades, Ireland seemed at peace in 1900. Wyndham's Land Purchase Act of 1902 (Wyndham was the Chief Secretary of Ireland from 1900) gave landless peasants loans at low interest repayable over 68 years. By 1910, 250,000 tenants had loans. There was also some devolved power.

In 1898 the county councils legislation had been extended to Ireland. There was no evidence of any violent future and 'killing Home Rule by kindness' appeared to have worked. This worked to the advantage of the Liberals. Without the issue that had divided them for so long, they could focus on other matters, such as social reform, or concentrate on attacking the Conservatives.

The Licensing Act (1904) alienated traditional Conservative supporters

The Licensing Act was unpopular. Brewers would receive compensation for loss of license, but it was to be a self-contributory scheme. This angered both the anti-drink lobby (who objected to any compensation) *and* the brewers. However, it is difficult to imagine how many voters this might have affected. The brewers had been staunch supporters of the Conservatives for decades, but they may have voted against the Party temporarily in 1905.

A lack of social reform was evident

Despite the Education Act (1902), Balfour continued Salisbury's philosophy of self-help. Germany, by contrast, had introduced sickness insurance (1883) and pensions (1889) and it wasn't even a democracy. At the turn of the century there was growing concern about the poor, through compassion or fear, but the Conservatives didn't tackle this issue. This may have lost them votes amongst the working class, but the poor couldn't vote until 1918, so they may not have considered the issue significant. In the 1890s, those in employment enjoyed higher wages than before, which led to a consumer boom. However, this was slowing down in the first decade of the 1900s. Indeed, after 1905, 'real wages' were actually falling.

Imperial defence was also a cause for concern

Sir John Fisher was appointed First Sea Lord and a third (Atlantic) fleet was created in light of new anxieties about Britain's security. A new battleship, the Dreadnought class, was designed (and launched in 1906) indicating the desire to maintain Britain's naval supremacy, which was seen as vital for the defence of the Empire and British trade. The army was also being reformed after the Boer War. A Royal Commission was established in 1903 and Lord Roberts reviewed the army's tactical performance. The desire to see greater efficiency in Britain's military record was in tune with public sentiment, but by 1905, the Boer War was already being forgotten by the electorate; they had, after all, won the war. The Entente Cordiale, a settlement of differences with France, was unlikely to be a vote winner, and the Anglo-Japanese Alliance of 1902 was of little concern to most people in Britain. Nevertheless, the Liberals revived their criticisms of Conservative 'complacency' in defence.

The Taff Vale Judgement angered many working-class voters

A railway strike in Taff Vale in 1900 ended in the defeat of the trade union. The courts, supported by the House of Lords demanded that the union pay the railway company compensation for 'damages' (loss of profit) which amounted to £23,000. The precedent this set was critical; unions would have to pay to go on strike and few could afford the maintenance of their members in the strike as well as meeting costs for damages when it was all over. This rendered strikes virtually impossible. According to the historian Lord Blake, this was the biggest factor in the Conservatives losing support and contrasted with the good relations established with the New Model Unions in the 1870s. Blake wrote: 'It is hard to believe that Disraeli would have made a similar error'.

The final stages of the Boer War provoked hostility
Criticisms of Kitchener's tactics in the Boer War were summed up by the speech made by W.T. Stead, a Liberal newspaper editor. He asked 'When is a war not a war?' and replied 'When it is conducted by methods of barbarism'. The Liberals took up the attack and challenged the Conservatives' approach to the war. The public felt that the war should have been fought according to the rules of 'civilised warfare'. There was even some sympathy for the Boer leader Christian de Wet. In fact, Kitchener's tactics in this guerrilla war, such as the destruction of property, had already been used in many African and Asian campaigns to prompt guerrillas into open battle. Removing the civilians from the countryside had been necessary, as they were supplying the Boer commandos. Although Kitchener gave them better conditions than his own soldiers endured, the image of concentration camps became a symbol of all that was mismanaged and immoral about the war.

The alleged 'Chinese slavery' affair played on fears and prejudices
Chinese labourers brought in to help with the reconstruction of the towns and mines of South Africa also became a subject of dispute. Fifty thousand had arrived in South Africa by 1905. The Liberals implied that the Chinese 'coolies' were paid so little they were virtually slaves. They also used innuendo to imply that because thousands of Chinese men were housed in barracks without their families this would lead to homosexuality. The 'Chinese slavery' slogan again highlighted the 'immorality' of the imperial enterprise in southern Africa. The dominions protested and trade unions in Britain feared that a similar influx of cheap labour might be introduced in the United Kingdom.

There was a sense of change at the end of the century
Perhaps it was simply a desire for change after 17 years of Conservative government that prompted the electorate to vote for the Liberals. A sense of change was marked by the start of a new century. The death of Salisbury (1903), Queen Victoria (1901), and Gladstone (1898) suggested that all the Victorian titans had gone. Even imperialist enthusiasm had cooled. When Sir Francis Younghusband invaded Tibet in 1904 to forestall Russian annexation, he was criticised by the government. The energetic imperial Viceroy of India, Lord Curzon, was recalled in 1905 when the proposed partition of Bengal aroused nationalist opposition.

The Tariff Reform Campaign was the most damaging episode before the election

The Tariff Reform Campaign was probably the single most important factor in the Conservatives' defeat. Chamberlain was unable to persuade his Cabinet colleagues to bring an end to free trade and introduce protection against foreign competition. He resigned from the Party and launched his Campaign of Tariff Reform. The Party was divided over the issue. Some were prepared to back Chamberlain's concept of 'imperial preference' where all states within the British Empire would enjoy a free trade union, but all foreign states would be charged import duties. However, other Conservatives were not prepared to abandon free trade. Balfour tried to compromise but this gave an impression of weakness. Chamberlain tried to drum up support by speaking to mass meetings. The Liberals pursued Chamberlain, arranging to speak at the same venues as he did. They reduced his argument to a simplistic formula: tariffs would mean the end of cheap food (a great deal of food was being imported) and voters would have to choose between the 'little loaf' of the Conservatives and the 'large loaf' of the Liberals. This concept was attractive to the voters. Robert Roberts, who lived in Salford before the war, wrote: 'This was politics we could understand!' Chamberlain's arguments were more complex. He pointed out that Britain was the only country without tariffs and that her economic position was not as strong as it had been in the 1850s. Then, she had been so strong, she could afford to ignore the competition of others. The old shibboleth of free trade reunited the Liberals. Anthony Wood wrote: 'On the anvil of Chamberlain's oratory, the Liberals were hammered into a unity they had lacked for twenty years'. L.C.B. Seaman concluded: 'Once again, Chamberlain had shown his obtuseness as a politician by plunging so precipitately into the whirlpool of controversy'.

A secret electoral pact also affected the Conservatives

In 1903, the Liberals and the new Labour Party secretly arranged that whenever there was a 'three cornered' contest, with a candidate for each of the leading parties, the Liberal candidate would stand down to allow the anti-Conservative vote to remain undivided. This would ensure that the Conservatives were defeated and that Labour would get some representation. The Liberals also agreed to assist in the funding of labouring men leading to their nicknames as 'Lib-Labs'; paid for by the Liberal Party but 'Labour' in their orientation.

Balfour miscalculated over the timing of the election

Balfour resigned in the hope of calling the election at the moment the Liberals were squabbling over the future of the Empire in December 1905. This was an error since the Liberal dispute was not serious. The election took place over one week and was completed in January 1906. The results were: Liberals, 400; Conservatives and Unionists 157; Irish, 83; Labour, 29. This was a complete reversal of the 1900 result.

It is interesting to note that Balfour lost his seat, although he remained Party leader until 1911, and that Chamberlain increased his majority. The result reflects the fact that the Conservatives had seemed to challenge some fundamental values of the British people. Cheap bread was threatened by the concept of Tariff Reform. The right to strike was jeopardised by the Taff Vale Judgement. Worst of all, there was no progress on social reform and no action to tackle poor housing, low wages and widespread ill health. It would be fair to say that Balfour was out of step with the new spirit of the 1900s. The Liberals used every opportunity to highlight the threat to free trade and it was this issue, more than any other, that caught the public imagination.

What was New Liberalism?

There was a strong feeling of a fresh start at the start of the century. Britain had a new monarch, Edward VII (1901–10), soon to be followed by George V (1910–36). The Liberals had a relatively unknown new leader, Sir Henry Campbell Bannerman, who, at 69, represented the New Liberal principles. He was a former businessman known affectionately as 'CB'. Overlooked by many historians, this unassuming but determined man reunited the party for its remarkable 1905 victory. Inside the new government there were further changes. Only one, Sir Edward Grey, was an aristocrat, all the rest were the 'new men' of middle-class background. Most were, in fact, lawyers: Asquith was the Chancellor; Lloyd George was President of the Board of Trade; Haldane was Minister of War. There were also surprises. John Burns, who had been the leader of the militant 1889 Dock Strike and former member of the SDF (the Social Democratic Federation, a Marxist group) was President of the Local Government Board. Of the MPs in support of the government, 29 were Labour and a further 24 Liberals represented miners' unions. This working-class backing led to concerns that the Liberals were being hijacked by socialists.

New Liberalism was a new way of thinking

New Liberalism adopted some new principles. The Victorian idea of self-help, or the categorisation of the 'deserving' and 'undeserving' poor was challenged. Poverty had, of course, been around a long time, but new reports highlighted the extent of the problem and revealed that it was far more serious than had been imagined. The paradox was striking: the richest and most powerful Empire in the world was still plagued by slums, financial hardship, inadequate diets and widespread disease amongst a third of its population. The implication was that there should be government help. In the nineteenth century, it was feared that state intervention would inevitably remove the rights of the individual which was the bed-rock of Liberalism. This idea was now changing, especially in light of the reforms of the 1870s and 1880s. Herbert Samuel wrote: 'Self-reliance is a powerful force, but not powerful enough to cure unaided the diseases that afflict society. Liberty is of supreme importance, but state assistance, rightly directed, may extend the bounds of liberty'.

The concept of 'New' Liberalism can be challenged
However, there were still shades of the Old Liberalism. In the economy, the old
ideas of *laissez faire* in industry, and free trade in commerce, were attacked.
Nevertheless, the Liberals were eager to protect property, and would have
defended old ideas of free trade whatever the contrary arguments. They strongly
advocated the old Gladstonian idea of equality of opportunity (which allowed the
best to strive and achieve) but still felt that individuals had to demonstrate their
enterprise. They called for efficient administration, often under the new
catchphrase 'national efficiency', but they did not completely abandon the
prudency of retrenchment. When the Royal Navy asked for more ships to keep
pace with German armaments, many Liberals resented the increased expenditure. There was a strong desire for army reform after the shock of the early
setbacks in the South African war, but Haldane was under pressure to make
savings too. When the British army went to war in 1914, it did not have the heavy
artillery which had been a strong recommendation after the Boer War.

Why was New Liberalism necessary?

There was fresh concern about the extent and effects of poverty
In 1889, Charles Booth investigated the extent of poverty in London, eager to
show that a figure of 25%, which was the accepted estimate, was erroneous and
far too high. In fact, he found that 30% of Londoners were at or below the poverty
line. Seebohm Rowntree later proved that York was in the same position.
Victorians had felt that poverty was a defect of character (especially laziness) and
that poor people lacked a drive to help themselves. In the Elizabethan period,
paupers were cared for by the parish and given 'outdoor relief' (work in
agriculture). In the 1834 Poor Law Amendment Act, workhouses had provided a
convenient way to absorb the increased population of poor, and their harsh
conditions acted as an incentive to work hard. Parishes were formed into 'unions'
served by one workhouse. However, Booth discovered that poverty was not down
to choice, but the result of industrial depressions and circumstances. However, the
Booth report has to be understood as a product of its time. Some of his categories
are moral, rather than economic, and the assumptions he made on what
constituted poverty were based on a family size of four people which was hardly
typical of the poorest families. Rowntree discovered that employed people's wages
were so low that they lived at a 'poverty level' and he recommended a national
minimum wage of 21s 8d (£1.08) per week.

Health was another motive for tackling poverty
There may have been other motives for acting in 1900, and not before. At the end
of the South African War, there was a Royal Commission (1903). The
Commission found that many potential recruits were undernourished and had
been rejected from military service on grounds of ill health. There was speculation

that the race was degenerating and therefore action had to be taken to deal with poverty. There was a feeling that physical health, and moral health (or 'character') went together. If Britain was faced with a European enemy, rather than the colonial adversaries of Africa and Asia, then it was felt Britain needed to address this decay. There was an economic side to this concern too. Britain's industrial expansion was continuing, but not at the same rate as Germany and the USA. They were catching up with Britain's industrial lead and the projection of the trends into the future indicated Britain would soon fall behind. This relative decline demanded greater productivity, which, in turn, meant a healthy workforce.

Ambition and fear may also have been motives for New Liberalism
There were other pressures for a change of programme. The growth of the Labour Party and the trade unions reminded the Liberals that there was a need to address the issues which affected the working classes. Failure to deal adequately with poverty, low wages and poor living conditions might persuade the working classes to vote on class lines for their own party. A number of socialist movements had sprung up across Europe, some of which were associated with violence. There was also an urgency about the need to bring in a minimum wage, pensions and insurance for accident and sickness at work. These provisions already existed in autocratic Germany, and it was somewhat embarrassing that an undemocratic state should seem more enlightened than a democracy. However, the threat from Labour should not be exaggerated for they were a tiny party in 1906. Establishing a reputation for social reform was really a method of making clear the distinction between Liberalism and Conservatism. However, it should be noted that Lloyd George and Winston Churchill wanted to establish reputations for their own political careers. There was, perhaps, no plan for a welfare state. Instead these men made a series of responses to public feeling and gestures of goodwill. However, this may be too cynical, particularly if one examines the Liberals' record of social reform between 1906 and 1914.

Lloyd George was a driving force behind New Liberalism
Lloyd George had been brought up amongst impoverished families in Wales. He was motivated by a strong sense of Welsh nationalism, and by a desire to alleviate the conditions of hardship he had observed as a young man. He was gifted with the skill of oratory, and appealed to audiences by using colourful imagery. He was a radical, and used the language of his class to attack inequality. He had enormous reserves of energy, and conveyed a real passion for change. Despite all his popularity and wit, and a highly successful record as war leader between 1917 and 1918, his sincerity has been doubted. After the war, Lloyd George had promised the returning soldiers a 'land fit for heroes to live in', but this failed to materialise. He claimed to be a radical and yet led a Conservative-dominated coalition even when the crisis of war was over. He claimed to favour peace but threatened war

with Ireland and with Turkey in 1922, a belligerence which cost him the premiership. Lloyd George was a skilful and persuasive negotiator. He prevented a railway strike in 1907 and brought the strike wave of 1910–13 to an end by restraint and conciliation. Lloyd George was an adept politician, and a stirring leader who was able to get things done, but he was also an opportunist and he was not entirely trustworthy.

The reforms of New Liberalism

Trade union legislation

▶ *Trade Disputes Act, 1906.* This overturned the Taff Vale Judgement. Liberals seemed eager to present their own bill on this before Labour did. The terms stated that unions could not be sued for striking, and peaceful picketing was legalised. Thus, this legislation indicates that reforms were being prompted by Labour, and the means were there for unions to go on strike, which contributed to the strike wave of the 1910–13 period. The Act could be criticised as making the unions too powerful and immune from the law.

▶ *The Trade Union Act, 1913.* This Act followed a case in 1909 called the Osbourne Judgement. Osbourne, a Liberal, objected to the payments of a 'political levy' from his union subscriptions. The Lords upheld his case and ruled that union members would have to opt in (contract in) to a scheme of paying for a political party. Trade unions had been automatically supplying Labour with funds, and this ruling affected the party's performance in the 1910 elections. Labour were keen to pressure the Liberals into reversing the judgement. The Liberals needed the support of Labour and therefore agreed to the Trade Union Act. This shows that the Liberals were dependent on Labour to some extent, particularly as the Liberals lost seats after the 1910 elections.

Provisions for the workers

▶ *Old Age Pensions, 1909.* Pensions allocated 5s a week (25p) to those over 70. This would negate the need for the old to go into workhouses. It was attacked by Labour as offering too little. Many would not survive to 70, since the average life expectancy was 65; those with poor diets throughout their lives would be less likely to reach the age of 70. Lloyd George calculated that the introduction of pensions would help to win by-elections and 'stop the rot' in the party. It was popular, but Lloyd George got the credit for all the work that Asquith had done (Asquith moved from Chancellor to Prime Minister on the death of Campbell Bannerman in 1908).

Merchant Shipping Act, 1906
The Merchant Shipping Act regulated standards of food and accommodation for crews. It was introduced by Lloyd George. He also passed the Patents Act (protecting inventors) and the Port of Land Authority (centralised control of docks).

Coal Mines Act, 1908
This established a maximum eight-hour day for miners, the first time the government had intervened directly in hours of work.

Minimum Wage Act, 1912
Local boards were established to fix minimum wages for miners in different seams and conditions. It was passed hastily at the end of a coal strike to satisfy workers. But it failed to address the need for a national minimum wage. It was established at 5s a day and 2s per day for boys.

Insurance Act, 1911
The National Insurance Act covered health and employment insurance and was a contributory scheme where government, employee and employer all paid a sum.

Provision for children
▶ *Young offenders.* Young offenders were to be tried in a juvenile court rather than an adult one. Borstals were established (to separate children from adult prisoners) and probation officers were appointed to care for the offender when he was discharged. In 1908 penalties were established for selling illegal and harmful substances to children (cigarettes, tobacco and alcohol).

▶ *Meals at school.* Free meals could be provided at schools from 1906. However, this Labour Bill was not made compulsory. In 1914 only half of the local authorities had taken up the measure, so in 1914 it was made compulsory by the Liberal government.

▶ *Medical inspections for children.* Compulsory medical inspections were established in 1907. Free treatment could be provided by local authorities, but as many ignored it, the government provided grants for the inspections from 1912.

▶ *Elementary school children were given guaranteed places.* In order to ensure progression in education for poorer children, elementary school children were entitled to 25% of all secondary school places.

Assistance to the unemployed or those in 'sweated industries'
▶ *Labour Exchanges, 1909.* Winston Churchill introduced Labour Exchanges to tackle unemployment. Although the idea was also promoted by William

Beveridge from an idea by Beatrice Webb, it was Churchill who got the measure through Parliament. As unemployment had risen sharply between 1908–9, the Exchanges were designed to help people find work in the areas of highest unemployment. In 1913, there were 430 Exchanges in Britain, but all were voluntary. Despite their limited numbers they worked very effectively.

▶ *Trade Boards Act, 1909.* The Trade Boards Act established a minimum wage for four 'sweated industries' (those where people were engaged in intensive labour) such as box and lace making, tailoring and chain making. Conditions in these jobs were poor and the National Anti-Sweating League had alerted the Liberals to the plight of those engaged in the work, especially women. Trade union organisation was difficult since most of the work was 'piece rate'. In 1913, the act was extended to six more industries, such as hat making, bringing the total number protected by the legislation to 400,000.

▶ *Shops Act, 1911.* Shop assistants were given a half-day holiday per week, but shopkeepers could reclaim the hours during the week.

Parliamentary reforms
▶ *The Parliament Act, 1911* reduced the power of the House of Lords after the Lords Crisis. The Lords lost their right to veto legislation, and effectively reduced their powers to a maximum delay on bills to two years.

▶ *Payment of MPs, 1911.* The payment of MPs meant working-class men could sit in the House of Commons independently, instead of needing sponsorship from the Liberals, or a private income. This legislation benefited the Labour Party more than it did the Liberals.

Were the reforms successful?
Any judgement of 'success' depends on what the aim was. Was the aim to gather working-class support? Was the aim to alleviate poverty? Or was it merely to create the conditions for a traditional 'equality of opportunity'? The reforms were certainly significant when taken together, if apparently limited on their own. Some steps were taken to tackle the conditions of the poor, but much time and energy was absorbed in fighting the House of Lords which was dominated by the Conservatives. Once this had been achieved, the Liberals had lost their majority in Parliament and were dependent on the support of Labour and the Irish Nationalists. Irish demands for Home Rule created a fresh round of controversy and further delayed the planned social reform programme. To make matters worse, increased demands for naval expansion to face a threat from Germany, diverted precious funds from the social reform agenda. However, there were still some issues which were not addressed.

▶ There was no reform of the Poor Law. In 1909, two Royal Commissions, chaired by John Burns, failed to abolish workhouses. There was therefore a dual system of state aid and the Poor Law, and this lasted until 1929.

▶ There was no assistance to agricultural labourers, who remained the worse-off workers in society.

▶ Real wages rose little, if at all, between 1910 and 1914. There was no progress towards a national minimum wage, except for the miners in 1912.

▶ Trade unions were unimpressed with their conditions and militant strike action increased between 1910 and 1913, although it had subsided by 1914.

▶ In 1914, the numbers rejected by the army on health grounds was proportionally the same as in 1900. This was due to a time lag; reforms for children and adults needed more time to be effective. The soldiers of later generations were healthier.

Verdict on New Liberal reforms: the establishment of a 'service state'
The legislation was a start. It was a pioneering effort and it would be wrong to criticise the Liberals for not constructing a 'welfare state'; this would come later, after the Second World War. The Liberal reforms, according to Jo Grimmond, were a foundation for later generations to build on. Arthur Marwick agreed, stating it was Labour that established the welfare state after 1945. Donald Read argued that the Liberals had built a 'social service state' (setting minimum standards) rather than a welfare state (with comprehensive standards). However, we should not assume that all the reforms for the poorest of society took place at national government level. Local councils were paving streets, laying down roads, creating drainage systems, providing electricity, gas and water. Local councils were employing policemen, architects, doctors, sanitary inspectors, accountants, firemen, and teachers. This was a golden age of local government and it transformed the face of Britain's towns.

The Liberals faced a number of difficulties between 1906 and 1914
The Liberals did not achieve all their aims because they ran into a series of obstacles in the period 1906–1914. They clashed with the House of Lords over the budget of 1909, there was some concern about their handling of suffragette militancy, there was severe labour unrest and strike action, there was sectarian strife in Ireland between 1912 and 1914. Overseas there was a deterioration of relations with Germany leading to the outbreak of the First World War. Some of these will be evaluated in the next chapter.

The 1909 budget and the House of Lords dispute

The Conservatives in the House of Lords rejected or altered several Liberal Bills at the turn of the century, yet had never once interfered in the Conservatives' ministries of 1895–1905. Since the Lords were not elected, preventing the elected, majority Liberal government from carrying out its reforms could be seen as acting beyond the spirit of the constitution. The Liberals regarded it as undemocratic. The argument about the relative powers of the Commons and Lords provoked a constitutional crisis.

There was a steady development towards confrontation

In 1893, the Second Home Rule Bill was defeated by the House of Lords on the grounds that it was unconstitutional. The Lords believed that it was their duty to prevent the break-up of the United Kingdom which Irish devolution threatened. In 1894, Lord Rosebery's measures were defeated, but the actions were justified by the House of Lords on the basis it was acting against a minority government. In the decade that followed, the Conservative government was not penalised, but in 1906, the Liberals found their measures blocked. Campbell Bannerman's Education Bill was rejected, as was the Plural Voting Bill. This last measure would have ended the ability of wealthy property holders to vote in more than one constituency and was seen as an attack on the Conservative Party by the Lords. In 1907, two Liberal Bills were rejected and two more amended. In 1908, the Licensing Bill (to reduce number of pubs) was presented. Edward VII advised the Lords to pass it, but they rejected it because the brewers were a powerful pro-Conservative lobby who stood to lose profits if the Bill was passed. The Lords also prepared to oppose the introduction of pensions, so Asquith packaged it as part of the budget, which, by precedent, had never been 'molested'.

The rejection of the budget provoked a constitutional crisis

In 1909, the Lords rejected Lloyd George's budget. This *was* unconstitutional but Lloyd George had been provocative. His plan had been to raise £15 million from taxation of the richest to pay for naval expansion, pensions, labour exchanges and other reforms. Land tax and death duties would tax the rich directly, and the whole package appeared to be a thinly disguised assault on the landed gentry. It increased income tax, it increased duty on car ownership and petrol, it placed higher taxes on tobacco and spirits and it introduced a supertax on those with incomes over £5,000 a year. Lloyd George stated that this was 'A War Budget: It is for raising money to wage implacable War against poverty and squalidness'. Yet he also remarked: 'I'm not so sure we ought to pray for it to go through. I'm not so sure we should hope for its rejection. It would give us such a chance as we shall never have again'. From April to November the debate raged. The Lords felt they had to fight. The Conservatives established a Budget Protest League and argued that the Liberal taxes were 'socialism by the back door'. They felt their class was under attack. A land tax, they believed, would be the preliminary to the nationalisation of land. Lloyd George responded by defining the Lords as 'Stately consumption of wealth produced by others' and he led a campaign of 'peers versus the people'. This was the language of class war and it greatly alarmed the middle classes. In November 1909, the budget passed through the House of Commons (379 to 149 votes). Edward VII advised that the Lords should let it through, but they didn't.

The Conservatives rejection of the budget raised important questions

Lansdowne, the Conservative leader of the Lords, argued that such a revolutionary budget should be put to a general election. Balfour, the Conservative leader in the Commons, defended this decision. He argued that the Lords were only exercising their role as 'Watchdogs of the constitution' against irresponsible laws. Lloyd George ridiculed this by saying the Lords were 'Mr Balfour's poodle'; doing Balfour's bidding for party political motives. Can we say that Lloyd George was to blame for this crisis? Not in the sense that the Liberals needed the money they asked for. Nor did they expect the Lords to reject a money bill. Historically, these had always been accepted. However, this was an attempt by Lloyd George to outflank the Lords. It was humiliating for the Conservatives to deny money for defence and for the poor, but they knew the proposals attacked them directly. The impasse between the two chambers created a constitutional crisis. The question was, who was more important: the Lords or the Commons?

The crisis worsened in 1910

In January, Asquith decided to fight an election on the budget. The 'peers versus the people' campaign was not that popular though, suggesting that the public rejected the simplistic slogans of class war. Indeed the Conservatives made a remarkable recovery. It may have been that the radicalism of the Liberals was actually counter-productive. The results of the election were: Liberals 275, Conservative-Unionist 273, Labour 40, Irish Nationalists 82. The results perhaps reflect that some safe seats lost by the Conservatives in 1906 had reverted back to them. Some middle-class voters had also been put off by Lloyd George's approach. John Redmond, the Irish Nationalist leader, saw advantage in the Liberal predicament. He decided to support the reintroduction of the budget in return for a new Home Rule Bill and the reduction in the power of the Lords (bearing in mind the only reason the last Home Rule Bill had not got through in 1893 was the opposition of the Lords). In April 1910, a Parliament Bill and a new budget were presented. Surprisingly, the Lords accepted the budget without opposition. This looked like a tactical decision, because it could be asked whether the Parliament Bill was still necessary. On the other hand, the Conservatives claimed that the election result had produced the verdict of the people.

The Liberals decided to press ahead with a reform of the Lords

Asquith wanted to make sure that the Lords would reflect his party as much as the Conservatives, and he wanted guarantees that the Conservatives would be unable to reject more bills in the future, so he asked Edward VII to create 250 new Liberal peers. The king would only do so if another election were fought on this precise issue. Asquith hesitated because he wasn't sure if the Liberals would win; the January result had been close. He was already dependent on Irish and Labour support and his majority was much reduced. At that point Edward VII died and George V was to be crowned King. Asquith therefore sought another solution. A conference was proposed in order to have a discussion over six months to decide on the powers of the Commons and Lords, but the Conservatives would not agree to a loss of power to reject a Home Rule Bill (which itself was a constitutional issue concerning the United Kingdom and the Empire). Asquith could not agree to this as he had already given his word to Redmond to introduce a new Home Rule Bill. Therefore, in November, a new Parliament Bill was presented. It passed through the Commons with Irish support, but it was rejected by the Lords. Asquith then met George V in secret to request 250 Liberal peers, but the King would only agree if the Liberals could win the next election. Once again, the Liberals went to the people. In December, the election results were: Conservative-Unionists 272, Liberals 272, Labour 42, and Irish 84. The Parliament Bill thus, with Labour and Irish support, went through the Commons and up to the Lords in May 1911.

The Lords were defeated in 1911

In July 1911, Asquith announced to the Commons the King's agreement to create 250 peers if necessary to get the Parliament Bill through. Asquith was howled down by shouts of 'traitor' from Conservative benches. Lord Hugh Cecil, Salisbury's son, led the attack. Asquith was unable to finish his speech, such was the feeling of betrayal. The Conservatives felt that Asquith had used the King to circumvent the parliamentary system. They also felt that the election result, a draw between the Liberals and Conservatives, was not an endorsement from the people for reform of the Lords. In the Lords, the Conservatives were divided about the Bill. They fell into two groups, the 'hedgers' and 'ditchers' ('hedge your bets' and go with the Bill, or 'last ditch stand' against it). In August, the hedgers won, if only to avoid being swamped by 250 Liberal peers. The Bill thus passed through the Lords 131 votes to 114. The Parliament Act terms were as follows:

▶ No finance bills could be rejected or amended. The Speaker would decide on the definition of a bill.

▶ General elections were to take place every 5 years, not every seven as previously.

▶ If the Lords rejected or amended any other bill three times, on its third reading it would pass anyway. This gave the Lords, in effect, a delay of up to two years.

Verdict on the Parliament Act: the Commons was paramount

The Lords thus lost their powers, but they could still neutralise the last two years of any government. In fact, the Lords did delay several bills after 1911, namely, the Irish Home Rule Bill, the Welsh Disestablishment Bill and the Plural Voting

Bill. However, George Dangerfield described the Liberals as follows: 'Flushed with one of the greatest victories of all time, from that victory, they never recovered'. This suggests that the Parliament Act was the last gasp of a party in its death throes. However, this is misleading. It was the outbreak of war in 1914 that prevented more legislation from being passed. If the war had not intervened, there was nothing to stop these bills, or others, getting through, except the monarchy. The monarch still had to give royal assent to every Bill. Nevertheless, the royal assent was never withheld. Charles I's refusal to do so had provoked a constitutional crisis in 1641, and ultimately a civil war. Today, the monarchy is the only institution though that could prevent a legal dictatorship.

Old Liberalism and New Liberalism compared

Liberalism in the nineteenth century had been dominated by the ideas of Gladstone

Gladstone had been brought up a Tory but led the Liberal Party from its formation in 1859 as a coalition of Whigs (on the right wing of the Party), Nonconformists and radicals (on the left) and the rest of the Liberals of the centre. This diversity meant that Gladstone's ideas and personality tended to be the unifying force of the Party. His slogans were peace, retrenchment (an avoidance of spending public money) and reform. During the nineteenth century this agenda had been popular and Gladstone formed four governments, but he became unpopular because of his attempts to give Home Rule to Ireland and his insistence on cuts in public spending when government intervention was needed to tackle poverty and improve national defence. Gladstone formed his last government in July 1892, but it was a minority because of the split in the Party. The Liberals had 273 seats, the Conservatives 268, with the Liberal-Unionists holding 47, whilst the Irish Nationalists held 81 seats. Gladstone was reliant on Irish support to form the government and so he had been compelled to introduce a Second Home Rule Bill. He had hoped that the 'Newcastle Programme' would have been more popular. It advocated Home Rule for Ireland, elections every three years, allotments for workers, new powers for district and parish councils, limited working hours, new liabilities for employers in the event of accidents at work, and payment of MPs. Philip Magnus, Gladstone's biographer, saw this programme as sheer expediency. It is interesting to see some of these ideas reappear in New Liberalism.

Gladstone left a legacy in the Liberal Party

The Home Rule Bill had narrowly passed the Commons with 309 ayes and 267 noes, but it failed in the Lords (419 to 41 votes). The Bill had taken eight months to get through the Commons and had been accompanied by stormy debates. Gladstone had wanted to fight a general election purely on the issue of the House of Lords' powers, but his Party and the Cabinet refused. Things did not improve for Gladstone after a Local Government Act in 1894 because a row developed over spending on the navy. Gladstone was out of touch with the idea that government spending was necessary. He resigned in March 1894 and died four years later. This titanic figure had governed his Cabinet colleagues firmly and he demanded a moralistic approach to all policy. He could be roused to storms of passion over issues he felt strongly about, such as Ireland. Lord Rosebery, by contrast, had more in common with the Conservatives than with Gladstone. Rosebery did, however, allow the introduction of death duties to be included in the 1894 budget but the Lords rejected it. Rosebery resigned and an election reduced the Liberals to 177 seats, but gave the Conservatives 340, the Liberal-Unionists (in the government) 71, and Irish Nationalists 82. Gladstone's passing seemed to resolve the issue of retrenchment, but the Conservative influence in the House of Lords, and the increased taxation of the wealthy through death duties was proposed long before the 1909 budget.

Some Liberal principles were unchanged
Old Liberalism therefore seemed to belong to an earlier epoch of British military, naval and economic supremacy. By the 1890s, Gladstone's retrenchment was out of fashion. Moreover, the Liberal record of social reform had been retarded by Gladstone's obsession with trying to get Home Rule for Ireland. Gladstone did not challenge the Lords' powers in 1893, even though he considered the idea after the rejection of the Home Rule Bill. However, certain Liberal ideas were unchanging. Above all, the Liberal Party still stood for the liberty of the individual and it still valued the concept of an individual's right to private property. These points clearly made Liberalism different from socialism which advocated collective ownership and the redistribution of wealth over the interests of the individual.

Conclusion: New Liberalism was the product of its age
There can be no doubt that New Liberalism was a fresh agenda, without completely severing its historical roots or its political principles. It was distinctive and bold in its attempt to tackle the vexed question of poverty, and in its long struggle to assert the elected House of Commons over the Lords. New Liberalism also faced new challenges from militant suffragettes and from the emergence of the new Labour Party. Labour was not yet the Party of the working class, the Liberals still claimed that title, but the Liberals saw the need to ally themselves with it.

Tutorial

Progress questions
1. Why did the Conservatives lose the election of 1905?

2. What was the primary driving force behind New Liberalism?

3. How successful were Liberal reforms in dealing with poverty?

4. What justification did the House of Lords use when opposing the 1909 budget?

5. What aspects of New Liberalism generated fear amongst the middle classes?

Seminar discussion
1. Was New Liberalism 'socialism by the back door'?

2. 'New Liberalism was doomed to failure from the start: too many interests wanted to maintain the *status quo*'. How true is this statement?

Practical assignment
1. Compile a list of reasons why the Conservatives lost the election of 1905. Compare it with another list of why the Liberals won. Which is the most important? Find evidence to support your views.

2. Did Lloyd George deliberately provoke the House of Lords with his 1909 budget?

Study tips
1. Memorising a list of reforms is not indicative of a good historian. It is far better to be able to *evaluate* each reform, and to *make judgements* on their success or failure collectively.

2. Make a note of the *context* in which these reforms were introduced. Make sure you have a good grasp of the motives for the legislation. Poverty, the ambitions of Lloyd George and Churchill, the ideology of New Liberalism (state intervention), the desire for 'National Efficiency' and the threat from Labour were the most important. Taking the first letter from these headings gives you the mnemonic 'PAINT'.

3. A mnemonic for the reforms is 'TOMMY MCMELTS IP'. Try it out.

7

The Crisis of Liberalism, 1910–1914

One-minute summary – The Liberal government faced a series of challenges in the period 1910 to 1914. Apart from its struggle with the House of Lords from 1909, there was militancy from some of the trade unions. A wave of strikes swept Britain because of angry protests against wage levels and working conditions. Some strikes attracted the sympathy of workers from other industries and there was a strong possibility that unions would form alliances to compel the government to step in on their behalf against employers. Anger also characterised the suffragette demonstrations, as frustration with a lack of progress boiled over into violence. In the short term this proved to be counter-productive to the women's cause. The same sort of determination characterised the people in Ireland who either supported or opposed the introduction of Home Rule. Both Ulstermen and Irish Nationalists took up arms in preparation for a civil war. However, the worst difficulty of all was the outbreak of war in Europe. Unable to tolerate German hegemony on the Continent, nor aggression against Belgium or France, Britain was forced to participate in the world's first total war. The measures that war demanded were to prove the greatest challenge to Liberalism.

In this chapter you will learn:

▶ how New Unionism and militant syndicalism challenged Liberalism
▶ how the struggle for women's suffrage developed
▶ how the Home Rule crisis left the United Kingdom on the brink of civil war
▶ what historical controversies have broken out over the fate of Liberalism.

New Unionism and militant syndicalism

British industry faced new difficulties after 1900
Each of Britain's staple industries, mining, textiles, agriculture and iron and steel, was faced by increasing foreign competition. In textiles, 80% of producers still used the older 'mule' spindles rather than the newer ring spindle. This, combined with cheaper foreign labour, was rendering British textiles less competitive. This situation was made worse by increasing mechanisation. In response, Britain exported more of its textiles to the colonies and less developed countries. As a result, Britain was still the leading textile producer in Europe in 1914, but its future was uncertain. Agriculture had stagnated since the 1870s, and, in 1895, 77% of wheat consumed in the United Kingdom was imported. There was little new investment and the number of people employed in agriculture was falling. In

the iron and steel industry, the USA and Germany had surpassed British production totals. The workforce nevertheless objected to the introduction of piece-rate work and the destruction of the privileges associated with craft skills. In mining, Britain exported less of its coal than the USA or Germany and couldn't make the profits these countries enjoyed. It suffered from a structural problem too. Many of Britain's small coal seams were unsuited to the biggest machinery and many older seams were being worked out. Two thirds of Britain's coal in 1913 came from pits established before 1875. Without investment, pits were not equipped with steel pit props, electrical haulage, or sufficient mechanical coal cutters. The other extraction industries, tin, lead and zinc were practically wiped out by foreign competition by 1890.

The British economy was not in decline, but in transition
It would be wrong to think that Britain's economy was in decline. Coal extraction, iron and steel production, and shipyard construction were at their peak before the First World War. The balance of payments, the profit of exports weighed against the cost of imports, produced a healthy surplus of £239 million in 1913. Britain's merchant fleet carried most of the world's goods, and the British Empire was the centre of the global trading network. South African and Australian gold had provided a lucrative reserve to back the world's standard currency, the pound sterling. Britain's economy was also diversifying with significant growth in the financial sectors of banking and insurance. The City of London was the world's most important stock market with a huge array of assets and investment opportunities. Even the staple industries could draw solace from the European arms race which stimulated greater demand for coal and steel. These factors suggest that Britain's economy was, in fact, adapting to the changed global circumstances in which it found itself. The huge mineral reserves of the North American continent, or the new technologies of the German economy, with its consequent capacity to dominate the central European market, meant that Britain's virtual monopoly of industrialisation was bound to be ended sooner or later. However, these changes were not without anguish and anxiety for the British workforce.

There was a wave of strikes between 1910 and 1911 across Britain
In February 1910, 30,000 miners in South Wales came out on strike because of anger at their working conditions. Such was the intensity of feeling that rioting broke out. Churchill delayed the despatch of troops to restore order, but in November, the Chief Constable of Glamorgan called them forward to deal with local disturbances in Rhondda and Aderdare. In July, railway workers went on strike on Tyneside and in September, 120,000 cotton workers were also on strike. The same month, as the Board of Trade settled the textile workers' dispute at Accrington, boiler makers in Newcastle began a strike that lasted until December. At bottom was the grievance that wages had stagnated at a time when prices were

rising. In June 1911, there was a ten-day strike of seamen and firemen. In Southampton, the shipping owners gave way, which encouraged the dockers of the Port of London to go on strike themselves in July. The eleven-day strike, involving 20,000 workers, was settled but in the north, similar industrial action led to rioting. On 15 August, two men were shot and killed by troops who had been brought in to quell the disturbances. On the same day, the Amalgamated Society of Railway Servants went on strike and most of the rail traffic of the north came to a standstill. As troops were called in to suppress more rioting, two more men were shot, this time whilst looting a shop and a train in Llanelli. In December, 126,000 weavers stopped working and were locked out. The dispute was settled by negotiation, but £1 million in wages was lost.

Syndicalist ideas coincided with the radicalism shown by the unions

The strike action of 1910–11 had been sporadic and uncoordinated, but syndicalist ideas from France suggested that unions were the real democracy of a country. The French model suggested that the unions should work together, using the sympathetic strike to force the employers into concessions. Older union leaders were troubled by this new radicalism as much as the government. There was concern that alliances of unions might turn their attention on the democratic system itself. Strikes might paralyse the country and hold elected governments to ransom. Some revolutionaries already speculated that a general strike of all workers could be used as a political weapon. It might even be used to dismantle capitalism altogether. The main advocate of this was Tom Mann, editor of the *Syndicalist* and the author of the influential text *The Miners' Next Step* (1912). Lloyd George, and George Askwith of the Board of Trade, had been tireless in arranging arbitration meetings between workers and their employers in an attempt to head off further crisis.

The strike action was not as serious in 1912 and 1913

In March 1912, the Miners' Confederation called a strike for a minimum wage. Two million workers were called out. The strike was resolved in April and the government granted the Minimum Wage Act. In May, the dockers again went on strike, but the government did not intervene and the action collapsed in June. In 1913, there was a strike by transport workers in Dublin and a series of small disputes in metal industries in the Midlands, but the worst was over. The threat of united action was still evident, however. The railway workers, miners and transport workers seemed poised to use a 'triple alliance' of their three organisations to strike and force the government to intervene on their behalf, but the strike never came. It wasn't until 1926 that the unions called for a general strike and the response, although encouraging, didn't produce the desired result.

The causes of the strikes were varied across the trades

The strikes were mainly the result of wages and prices being out of step, a situation that began to improve after 1913, but the government was forced to react to the industrial action of the workforce. It was identified that some of the grievances were very specific to the trades concerned. New technology displaced workers, adjustments caused friction between employees and between workers and employers, unemployment in some industries had fallen and consequently increased the bargaining power of the workforce, and there was the fierce blast of foreign competition making greater demands in efficiency. However, the Liberals had inadvertently made the strike wave possible by the Trade Disputes Act. The legal position of unions had been challenged by the Taff Vale Judgement, but the extent of union power had not been established.

The government's responses were generally fair, if limited
The Liberal government was hardly in a position to be able to control the great forces of supply and demand at work in the global marketplace, nor the adjustments occurring in the British economy. Rocked by the stormy symptoms of change, and the hardships that resulted from the loss of Britain's industrial leadership, there was little that the Liberals could do except encourage negotiations between employers and employees. Askwith, the Chief Industrial Commissioner from 1911, did precisely that. Conciliation Boards were established and numbered 325 in 1913. A national industrial council was set up to bring together employers and trade union leaders. The government was also determined to maintain law and order, using the army where necessary.

The challenge of the suffragettes

The origins of the cause of women's suffrage can be traced back to 1867
Following the rejection of John Stuart Mill's proposal that women should be given the vote in 1867, women's suffrage societies sprang up in London, Manchester and Edinburgh. The following year, denied the chance to vote at the general election, new groups were formed in Birmingham and Bristol. In 1873, and again in 1888, petitions were presented to Parliament, but in 1889, the journal *Nineteenth Century* published a counter petition against women's suffrage, by other women. By 1900, the various suffrage groups came together under the leadership of Millicent Fawcett in the National Union of Women's Suffrage Societies. This was a moderate organisation which aimed to see the extension of existing legislation. In 1875, women could be elected to School and Poor Law Boards. In 1888, women could vote in municipal, county council and county borough elections. It seemed only a matter of time before women would be granted the same voting qualifications as men, that is, ownership of property.

There were economic and social changes which prompted a growth of interest
A shift in the employment pattern of women mirrored the broader pattern of change in the British economy. Fewer women were finding employment on the land or in mining. Middle-class women were eager to take up the new tertiary

sector jobs of clerks and secretaries in banking, insurance, commerce and the civil service. Domestic service remained the primary occupation for many working-class women, but the educated few were gaining the more prestigious employment as doctors so that, by 1900, there were 100 in this part of the medical profession. Florence Nightingale's Crimean service had popularised the idea that nursing was also suitable for women. By the turn of the century there were 70,000 nurses. In total, five million women were earning wages by 1900. These changes were the result of the enormous demand for workers in the tertiary sector, and the product of the educational reforms of the 1870s and 1880s. The combination of demand and education was probably as significant as the political changes that had taken place between 1867 and 1888. The Liberal government was sympathetic to the plight of poorer women, particularly after the match girls' strike in 1888. Their Trade Boards Act (1909) established a minimum wage in the sweated industries which included those women who made matches. It therefore seemed likely that the Liberal government would look favourably on franchise reform too.

What were the aims of the suffragettes?

In 1903, the WSPU (Women's Social and Political Union) was formed by the militant leader, Emmeline Pankhurst. They rejected the moderate tactics of the suffragists, and differentiated themselves by the title 'suffragettes'. Pankhurst was schooled in the art of protest and opposition throughout her life. She had served on the committee that had promoted the Married Women's Property Act with her husband, and it was her husband, a friend of James Stuart Mill, who had shaped Pankhurst's political outlook. In 1889 she formed the Women's Franchise League, but it had collapsed. She left the Liberal Party and joined the Independent Labour Party in 1892. It was her daughter's views that reawakened an interest in the cause of women's suffrage and the establishment of the WSPU. The militancy developed almost straight away. Christabel Pankhurst and Annie Kenney tried to challenge Sir Edward Grey at a meeting in the Manchester Free Trade Hall. Their heckling aroused some hostility from the audience. They were ejected, allegedly spitting and punching the policemen who forced them out. Refusing to pay fines for 'disorderly conduct', they were sent to prison. From this point, the aim was to force the government to make concessions through disruption. Pankhurst knew that the press would report on WSPU activities, and she used this to her advantage.

The early tactics of the suffragettes aroused opposition

In 1906, Pankhurst led groups to the House of Commons which resulted in clashes with the police. More members of the WSPU were imprisoned. She organised a march in London, but there was ridicule from many of the onlookers. Later marches resulted in more arrests. In January 1908, she was pelted with eggs and rolled in mud by angry crowds at Newton Abbot. In February she was arrested whilst carrying a petition to Parliament, but she only served a few weeks of her sentence. She was arrested again in October but soon organised a protest within Holloway Prison claiming that she and her followers should be treated as 'political prisoners'. In 1909, the WSPU began hunger strikes which prompted the prison authorities to force-feed WSPU members to keep them alive. Suffragettes turned this into a propaganda exercise, and claimed that their members were being ill treated. Pankhurst, only recently released, was arrested again at the doors of the Commons. Whilst waiting for an appeal she made a lecturing tour of America and her fines were paid by an unknown benefactor. Pankhurst later wrote that she had: 'declared war, not only on all anti-suffrage forces, but on all neutral and non-active forces'. If the aim was to attract attention, then this was being achieved, but it was at the expense of goodwill and sympathy from the general public.

The suffragette campaign became more extreme
The WSPU stepped up their violence by smashing windows in the infamous 'toffee hammer' attacks. Whitehall, Downing Street and many London clubs were subject to this vandalism, but when this failed to move the government, schools, houses and a railway station were set on fire. Paintings in art galleries were slashed, bombs detonated (including Lloyd George's home), burning rags were dropped into letter boxes and Asquith was beaten with iron golf clubs at Lossiemouth. Pankhurst was again arrested and sent to prison, immediately going on hunger strike, and later, a thirst strike. The campaign had become so extreme that Pankhurst seemed to court death, and it is possible that she encouraged martyrdom. Emily Davison certainly felt this way. Having laid a wreath at Joan of Arc's statue, she threw herself beneath the King's horse on Derby Day in 1913. Ann Morley and Liz Stanley argued that the suffragettes were careful to avoid physical harm to others, even though they sustained injury themselves. They criticise the police for 'physical and sexual assault' and draw attention to the legitimacy of the WSPU cause. Yet Pankhurst's claim that the general public were being won over to the cause seems to be an exaggeration. The Prisoners Temporary Discharge Act (1913), or the 'Cat and Mouse Act' as it was called, was designed to release hunger strikers long enough to permit recovery before re-arresting them. This measure did alarm the public for it seemed cynical and illiberal, but it was thought of as a necessary measure given the extremism of the suffragettes.

Did the suffragettes achieve anything?
Martin Pugh believed that the only achievement of the suffragettes was an awareness of the WSPU's beliefs. They did not win the vote. In fact, they alienated a great number of sympathetic politicians in the Liberal Party. The government refused to be moved by WSPU tactics. In 1907, the Cabinet had agreed in principle with the idea of women's suffrage, but felt that, whilst men without property had no vote it would prove too unpopular to give women the vote. Married men, for example, from the poorest families, would not be able to

vote, whilst young unmarried women could, and this seemed to be illogical when measured against the degree of responsibility they exercised. The WSPU also failed to represent the interests of working-class women. Indeed, by 1914, the movement was split and the loyal rump was characterised only by an unstinting loyalty to the Pankhursts. When, during 1916 and 1918, the idea of women's suffrage was being debated, the Pankhursts had abandoned the campaign. None of them returned to the issue after the war. Emmeline Pankhurst visited Russia in 1917, but turned against Bolshevism and it may have been this that convinced her not to take up the militant, revolutionary cause again in the 1920s. The WSPU's tactics had caused the Liberal government some irritation and it was, in the words of Anthony Wood: 'a psychological revolt, a state of war declared on the whole Victorian world of men'.

The question of Home Rule for Ireland, 1912–1914

The Home Rule crisis was the most serious
The Conservatives and the House of Lords took up Ulster's cause and warned that Home Rule would lead, first, to the break up of the United Kingdom, and then to the collapse of the Empire. In 1914, even though a Home Rule Bill had passed the Commons and the Lords, Ulstermen and southern Irishmen prepared to fight a civil war. This was the largest and most serious crisis the Liberals faced before the outbreak of the Great War.

The Third Home Rule Bill led to preparations for a civil war
When the House of Lords lost its powers of veto in 1911 and the Liberals introduced the Third Home Rule Bill the following year, the Ulstermen threatened that they would form their own provisional assembly. Andrew Bonar Law, the Conservative leader, strongly supported the idea. At Blenheim Palace in 1912 he announced that 'I can imagine no lengths of resistance to which Ulster will go, which I shall not be ready to support'. In other words, the leader of His Majesty's Opposition was prepared to back the use of force to resist the decision of Parliament. The Conservatives felt that the Liberal Bill was unconstitutional. The fact that the Liberals were dependent on Irish Nationalists to stay in power only served to reinforce their conviction that the Liberals were playing party politics with the nation's future. The Conservative-Unionist bond had been established in 1886 when the First Home Rule Bill had been presented, but now the alliance appeared a necessary fact. The Ulstermen were not prepared to rely solely on their political allies though. They began to arm themselves for the arrival of the inevitable Act.

Asquith adopted a policy of 'wait and see'
Curiously, Asquith, the Liberal Prime Minister, decided not to act against this private army. He seems to have believed that the Conservatives did not really

intend to carry out their threat and decided to 'wait and see' what events occurred in Ireland itself. It was not until March 1914 that Asquith realised he might have to arrange for the exclusion of Ulster from the Act. He failed to move against the Ulster Volunteers, or deal with the gunrunning which had begun on Ireland's coasts. In response, southern Irishmen began to form volunteer units of their own. It seemed that a civil war was imminent.

There was doubt about the position of the army and police

In March 1914, Asquith decided to send troops to Ulster to defend key installations. However, the senior officers at the Curragh barracks near Dublin made it known that they would resign rather than fight against their own countrymen. Seeley, the Secretary of State for War, actually accepted this decision, promising that the army would not be used in this way. Asquith promptly removed Seeley, but it was unclear what the army's role would be. In April, 30,000 rifles were brought in by the Ulster Volunteers. The police took no action even though such activity had been declared illegal.

The failure of negotiations made civil war more likely

George V summoned the leaders and proposed a conference at Buckingham Palace in the summer of 1914. Redmond, the nationalist leader, agreed that Ulster should be excluded from the provisions of the Home Rule Bill, but changed his mind when it was revealed that Ulstermen wanted Fermanagh and Tyrone included in the definition of 'Ulster'. These counties were 50% Catholic. The conference ended in July without a decision. On 26th July, Irish Volunteers smuggled 1,500 rifles into Ireland, despite the patrols of the army. At Howth, the crowd stoned the troops and they retaliated leaving three dead and 38 wounded. The outbreak of the Great War interrupted further negotiations and preparation for civil war. Redmond called on Irish Nationalists to fight for the Empire, expecting Home Rule as their reward and 150,000 volunteered. Ulstermen formed their own division, the 36th, which distinguished itself many times during the Great War.

There was a sense of desperation amongst Unionists between 1912 and 1914

The lack of decisive leadership by Asquith between 1912 and 1914 merely encouraged the Ulstermen to shape their own destiny. It is a paradox that the Irish Volunteers were prepared to fight to implement an Act of Parliament, whilst those who claimed the greatest loyalty to the Crown and the United Kingdom were advocating armed resistance. This claim to loyalty was tested to the limit, not in Ireland, but on the battlefields of France and Flanders. Irish soldiers, from north and south, proved that loyalty many times between 1914 and 1918. Andrew Bonar Law, who was a largely unknown force in British politics, couldn't really oppose the massive Liberal majority of the Commons to prevent Home Rule. The Lords were used to delay legislation in the hope that the Liberal government would reconsider its position, or perhaps were defeated in an election. Bonar Law could be accused of encouraging Loyalist resistance by stating his support for the Ulstermen against Irish Home Rule. However, his view was entirely in keeping with Conservative ideas on the preservation of the United Kingdom and the Empire. After the Parliament Act, the Conservatives felt besieged by the Liberals and their reaction, although extreme, can only be understood against this background. They felt, as did the Ulstermen, that the future of their country was at stake.

Historical controversies

The strange death of Liberal England

George Dangerfield's view, in *The Strange Death of Liberal England* (1936), was that Liberalism died in the period 1910 to 1914. He argued that the workers could no longer tolerate the Victorian respectability which held them in their class position, and they revolted through the strike wave of 1910–1913. He described: 'the deepest impulse... of 1910–1914 was an unconscious one, an enormous energy pressing up from the depths of the soul; and Parliament shuddered before it and under its impact Liberal England died'. The implication was that a new form of mass politics had replaced the old assumptions about the paramountcy of individualism. G.L Bernstein (1986) argued that liberalism was unable to adapt to the interests of the working class and it was only a matter of time before the Liberal Party was replaced by Labour. However, P.F. Clarke (1971) pointed out that class consciousness was highly developed by 1910, but Labour were still small and the Liberals still in power. Clarke believed that the expectation was that Labour and the Liberal Party would 'be subsumed into progressivism', coalescing into the same movement.

The views of Trevor Wilson, Duncan Tanner and Martin Pugh

Trevor Wilson (*Downfall of the Liberal Party*, 1966) drew an analogy between the Liberal Party and an old man. He argued that after a period of great exertion, he had suffered illness (the suffragette disruption, the industrial disputes of 1910–13 and the Home Rule crisis). Then he was hit by a 'rampant omnibus, which mounted the pavement and ran him over', which Wilson suggested was the First World War. Wilson believed that, however important the 'illness' was, it was 'the bus', the war, that killed him. Tanner used a less colourful style to show that the Liberals' replacement by Labour was not inevitable before the war. The Liberals had been able to hold together a coalition of working-class and middle-class interests and it was their attitude to the war, and a party split in 1916, that led to their defeat in the 1918 election. Pugh agreed that the war was the most important factor, but he highlighted the pre-war weaknesses too. He argued that the progressive social reform programme made the Liberals strong as long as it continued and the war interrupted it. Yet before that, the need for state intervention cut across the old principles of Liberalism and this began to alienate the middle-class supporters. Taken together, historical interpretations have tended to conclude that the Liberals' rout after the war was caused either by their replacement by Labour, the impact of the First World War, or by ideological weaknesses in New Liberalism.

Tutorial

Progress questions
1. Why were the unions more militant between 1910 and 1913 than before?

2. What changes were taking place in the British economy and employment patterns for women?

3. How well did the Liberals cope with suffragette agitation between 1906 and 1914?

4. How far did Asquith's actions worsen the crisis in Ireland between 1912 and 1914?

5. Why do historians refer to a 'strange death' of Liberalism?

Seminar discussion
'The contradictions of Liberalism were revealed by the way the government dealt with suffragettes, trade unions and the Ulstermen.' Do you agree?

Practical assignment
Make a note of the historians' views on the 'decline' of Liberalism. Match these views against the events of 1906–1914. What were the Liberals most important weaknesses? What was strong or skilful in their dealings with the crises of 1910–1914?

Study tips
1. The question of Liberal 'decline' has provoked a great deal of controversy. It is important to acknowledge this debate. Try to make a note of the evidence used to support each interpretation and use this in your own work.

2. Try to avoid value judgements over the WSPU; this is an emotive issue which still provokes a lively debate. It is important to remain detached and non-partisan if your views are to be persuasive and convincing.

3. Bear in mind that the events in this chapter, although divided up for clarity, all occurred simultaneously. A citizen in 1912 would have been aware of the coincidence of troubles in Ireland, suffragette agitation, the recent controversy over the Parliament Act and strike action.

8

Labour Politics, 1893–1914

One-minute summary – Labour's emergence, from a handful of theorists and activists to a mass party, is a remarkable history. Against a political system based on property and wealth, the independent candidates, with growing trade union support, gradually established themselves. At first they relied on the Liberals, and, indeed, before 1914, their survival seemed uncertain. Yet it is a testament to the British system of parliamentary democracy that the country could accommodate MPs with a socialist philosophy. Labour themselves assisted in this assimilation by advocating peaceful and gradual change. Elsewhere in Europe, democratic socialist parties were viewed as agents of revolution.

In this chapter you will learn:

▶ how the Labour Party originated
▶ who led the Labour Party
▶ what the aims of the Labour Party were
▶ the significance of the Labour movement
▶ the verdict on the Labour Party in 1914.

The origins of the Labour Party

The Independent Labour Party was created in 1893 at the Bradford Conference from three groups. The Social Democratic Federation, formed in 1884, favoured the creation of a socialist society through revolution and they were essentially Marxist in outlook. The Fabian Society, also formed in 1884, was made up of intellectuals like Beatrice and Sydney Webb. Their approach was moderate, even theoretical, rather than revolutionary. In the north of England, working-class men had formed their own associations, such as the North of England Socialist Federation (1887), the Bradford Labour Union (1891) and the Manchester Independent Labour Party (1892). It was this title that the party, under the chairmanship of Keir Hardie, adopted in 1892 and maintained until 1900. In February 1900, an alliance was formed with the trade union movement and the organisation was renamed the Labour Representation Committee. The title reflected the dominance of the unions. It had been the TUC (Trades Union Congress) that called forward the ILP and the LRC was not regarded as a political party as such, more of a platform for parliamentary pressure. However, many unions chose not to affiliate with the LRC preferring to back the Liberals. The greatest support came from the unions that represented unskilled labourers. The dock strike of 1889, the gas workers strike of 1889–90 and the match girls' industrial action reflected a new organisation amongst unskilled workers. They were unhappy with the 'closed shop' of established 'skilled' unions, and disappointed by the lack of social reform in the 1890s.

The Party was dependent on the unions
In 1900, the LRC was woefully short of funds and political experience. The diversity of its membership meant that it was difficult to identify a common programme. In the 'khaki election' of 1900, the LRC polled 63,000 votes and returned two MPs to Parliament. Although this was a small beginning, it was noticeable that trade union membership was growing steadily. In 1871, the TUC had 289,000 union members. The total membership of trade unions had grown to 1.5 million by 1892 and in 1900, there were 2,022,000 members. The most rapid growth of the unions occurred after 1910: 2.56 million to 4.14 million in 1914. Moreover, the unions provided most of Labour's funds. The unions were thus the key to Labour's future success and they dominated the LRC with a block vote.

Keir Hardie was the founding father of Labour
Keir Hardie is credited with being the 'father of the Labour Party'. He was born in 1856 and came from a poor background. He was a trade unionist and journalist who stood for election in London in 1892. He founded the ILP and helped negotiate the alliance with the unions to form the LRC. He was the Party Chairman at the foundation of the Labour Party, a title it adopted in 1906. Hardie remained MP for Merthyr Tydfil between 1900 and 1915 but bitterly opposed Britain's participation in the Great War.

Ramsay MacDonald has been regarded as a schemer
MacDonald also endured an upbringing in poverty, and joined the ILP in 1894. He negotiated the secret electoral pact of 1903 with the Liberal Party which ensured that LRC candidates were not opposed by Liberals. He was elected in 1906 and took over the chairmanship of the Party in 1911. He resigned in 1914 because he opposed the war. After the war, MacDonald became the first Labour Prime Minister in 1924, and again in 1929. He was severely criticised by party colleagues for abandoning the party in 1931 to form a National Government in the midst of an economic crisis. Labour historians have often sought the roots of this 'betrayal' in his early career.

The aims of the Labour Party

Labour ideology was a mixture of utopianism, socialism and pragmatism
For the intellectuals and theorists, Labour was the first step in a long road towards a better society. William Morris of the arts and crafts movement was already experimenting with social equality amongst small groups of independent artisans. However, Morris' idyll owed more to the conception of a pre-industrial era where

Policy	Liberals	Labour
Poverty	Recognition in 1906 that poverty had to be tackled and a minimum standard of care had to be established.	Labour eager to eradicate poverty by changing the social and economic system: state ownership of all industry would ensure wealth was redistributed to the needy.
Political power	Liberals aimed to preserve the constitution but to meet the needs of the working classes and the poor through the existing system. They used the language of class politics to win support.	Labour wanted to change the political system but not by revolution. Eventually they wanted all men and some women to be able to vote. They also used the language of class politics. Labour had been formed because it felt the other parties were not meeting their needs.
Decline and rise	Some see the fall of the Liberals as inevitable. Others argue that it was specific problems that the Liberals could not solve such as crisis of leadership brought on by the war.	The Labour Party was struggling at first, but it was able to show that it was moderate and put pressure on the Liberals to reform the country.

Fig. 5. New Liberalism and Labour compared.

each man enjoyed the fruit of his own labour and craftsmanship was highly valued. It was little more than a reaction to the mass-production of a consumer society, and it was this that characterised Britain in 1900. There is little doubt that socialism was more influential and it came from a number of sources. Hyndman, the SDF leader, espoused revolution along the lines of Karl Marx's doctrine, but it was the Fabians who attracted more sympathy because they advocated change via the existing political system. Sydney Webb, for example, served on London's council. Keir Hardie was less interested in the theory of socialism, than in the practical business of making changes happen. He regarded socialism as 'life for the dying people' and tried to persuade the Liberals to bring about social reforms. Nevertheless, the programme was essentially 'collective ownership of the means of production, distribution and exchange'.

Labour was a cautious movement
Despite Labour pressure to bring about the Trades Disputes Act, criticisms of pensions and Labour Exchanges (which they feared would mean the more efficient arrival of 'blackleg' workers during a strike) and their own free school meals legislation, many members of unskilled unions were disappointed with Labour. Some workers were put off by the doctrinaire attitude of the party, others turned to syndicalism to produce results.

Labour did not fare well before 1914
In 1906, despite the unpopularity of some Conservatives policies and the secret pact with the Liberals, the LRC gained only 29 seats out of 51 candidates. In 1910, the Osbourne Judgement (1908) had depleted party funds and they gained

40 seats in January, and 42 in December. Nevertheless, some of these MPs were originally Lib-Labs who had transferred to the Labour Party, so the actual increase was much smaller. Indeed, after by-elections, the party was down to 36 seats by 1914. Beatrice Webb believed that the Liberals' social reforms removed the need for a Labour movement. She stated that Churchill and Lloyd George had taken the limelight. She was particularly disappointed by the congratulation Labour MPs gave themselves for pressuring the Liberals into reform, and despaired that there was division within the Party. She described Hardie as 'used up', Snowden as 'bitter, apathetic and ill', and MacDonald 'almost preparing for his exit from the ILP...to join the Liberal Party'. She felt that the rank and file were disillusioned. The party split in 1914 over participation in the war, Henderson leading the group that supported the war effort.

The significance of the Labour movement

The very existence of a working-class movement was still significant

Labour's achievements, although modest, indicated that at least a minority of the working classes felt distinct from the middle-class politicians and their policies in this period. They were not 'alienated' in the classic Marxist sense, and thereby ripe for revolution, but they did want to establish their own identity and put forward issues which mattered to them. Labour leaders generally came from the same background as those they represented. They knew at first hand what poverty meant. It was also unlikely that the Liberals could really fully understand this when, as Christopher Harvie and H.C.G Matthew put it they 'would not adopt as candidates men whom they would expect to enter their houses by the servants' door'.

The verdict on the Labour Party in 1914

With the benefit of hindsight it is easy to assume that the rise of Labour was inevitable, but it was not. During the war, Henderson was invited by Asquith to support the government and so bring all the unions behind the war effort. Barnes served in the War Cabinet under Lloyd George and it was through these means that Labour gained valuable government experience. In 1924, they formed a minority government at the request of Stanley Baldwin. The Conservatives had won the election, but Baldwin was eager to assimilate Labour into democratic politics lest they become alienated and revolutionary. It was not until 1929, after these experiences that they formed a popular government and truly replaced the Liberals as the party of opposition. Before the war the situation had been very different. Labour was a small party, short of funds (until the reversal of the Osbourne Judgement in 1913), and concerned that the Liberal social reforms were the *raison d'être* of the movement. However, Labour wanted to see Britain move gradually towards a form of society that offered more to the working classes. Eventually they wished to see state ownership, because they believed it was the only system that could guarantee greater equality. Above all, they wanted to be free of the poverty that burdened one third of the British people. However, it was the unions that offered the best prospect of change. Strikes had ended with government conciliation, unions had proved immense solidarity existed between and within unions, and, during the war, the unions saw the extension of state ownership.

Tutorial

Progress questions
1. To what did Labour owe its origins?

2. Why were the unions the most important part of the Labour movement?

3. Why was the Labour Party in difficulties before 1914?

4. What was the most significant aspect of the Labour Party's existence?

Seminar discussion
Did the Labour Party really represent the working classes before 1914?

Practical assignment
List the ideas, groups and leaders of the Labour movement. How revolutionary was the organisation in its methods and ideas?

Study tips
1. Try to avoid using the benefit of hindsight to try to understand the problems Labour faced before 1914.

2. Think of the reasons why Labour were not popular, as well as the factors that attracted support. This will be useful material for a counter-argument to the 'inevitability' approach.

3. Be aware that the decline of the Liberals and the rise of Labour are often considered together.

9

Foreign Policy and International Crises, 1902–1914

One-minute summary – Britain's imperial strength had been challenged in the South African War, and, despite victory in 1902, there was concern that if Britain had difficulty in winning a colonial conflict, it would be hard pressed to defeat a European adversary. The dispersed nature of the Empire was its fundamental weakness: the combined threats of Germany, France and Russia could not be contained all over the world. Rosebery had speculated that, if Britain was to defend every imperial interest that was under threat, it would find itself fighting forty wars at once. This was an exaggeration, but it captured the mood of the period. Although Britain settled its differences with Russia and France, a new antagonism developed with Germany. Threats to the British Empire and to Britain's naval supremacy (and therefore the security of trade and the import of foodstuffs), coincided with a series of international disputes which together persuaded the War Office and the Admiralty to consider closer co-operation with France. Initially, Britain's only involvement in the July Crisis of 1914 was an attempt to set up an international conference to preserve peace, but the German invasion of neutral Belgium compelled Britain to go to war.

In this chapter you will learn:

▶ how Britain ended its isolation in 1902
▶ how Germany emerged as a new rival to Britain
▶ what caused the outbreak of the First World War.

The end of Britain's isolation

Britain ended its dangerous isolation in the Far East in 1902

In 1902 Britain concluded the Anglo-Japanese Alliance. It prompted a Liberal politician to exclaim: 'Our magnificent isolation has come to an end with a sudden shock'. However, it was a logical reorganisation of the defence of Britain's interests in the Far East. Russia was the primary cause for concern. She was annexing a considerable amount of territory in the Far East, and, by 1901 seemed to be the most important military and naval power of the region. The relative naval strengths of the Great Powers in the Far East was as follows:

	France	Russia	Britain	Japan
Battleships	1	5	4	6
Cruisers	2 (both old)	6	3 (2 old)	7 (new)

A.J.P. Taylor believed the Japanese Alliance was logical

A.J.P. Taylor wrote that whilst the bulk of the British army was involved in the South African War, whilst France was hostile after the Fashoda Incident, whilst Germany was unwilling to commit herself to an alliance against Russia (and happy to see Russia expand in Far East rather than interfere in Balkans or Europe), Japan was the only friendly power. An alliance with Japan didn't commit Britain against any European powers, and it gave her added naval strength in the Far East. Although Lansdowne wrote: 'Isolation is out of date', A.J.P. Taylor, however, argued: 'The alliance [1902] did not mark the end of British isolation, rather it confirmed it. Isolation meant aloofness from the European balance of power and this was now more possible than before'.

Britain and France settled their differences in 1904

The balance of power in the Far East was changed dramatically by the Russo-Japanese War. Japan attacked the Russians without warning in 1904, complaining that Russia had put Japanese security at risk by the annexation of Korea. Crucially for Britain, Russia could have called on its ally, France, to assist. If she did, under the terms of the Japanese Alliance, Britain would have to join in on Japan's side. Already considering closer relations, Delcasse (the French Foreign Minister) and Chamberlain, and then Lansdowne, had begun talks. The Russo-Japanese War speeded up the process and produced an Entente, or settlement of differences (February 1904). Edward VII's visit in May 1903 had already been a great public relations success. When he arrived in Paris he was heckled, but when he left, he was acclaimed. He was dignified, and his genuine love of France charmed the public. Although Britain and France agreed to mutually respect their spheres of influence in East and West Africa, the Entente Cordiale implied that other colonial disputes were now at an end. An immediate benefit was the French negotiations after the Dogger Bank Incident in October 1904. Russian ships sank British trawlers in the North Sea thinking they were Japanese torpedo boats, but the affair did not lead to war between Russia and Britain. However, Russia's defeat in 1905, and her paralysis by revolutionary insurrection at home, offered its rival Austria new opportunities in the Balkans.

Russia had been a major threat in Asia

Railway development for commercial and military purposes freed Russia from its physical difficulties of vast distances, and made possible the exploitation and development of continental hinterlands. By the 1890s Russia was challenging Britain's strategic position in Asia. The Trans-Siberian railway was designed to 'revolutionise world trade, supersede the Suez Canal as the leading route to China, enable Russia to flood the Chinese market with textiles and metal goods, and secure political control of northern China'. It was feared that railways would render Britain's naval supremacy irrelevant in the future as far as the defence of India was concerned. In 1901, it was calculated that India would require a garrison of 300,000 men, and the British army, in addition to its other commitments, would need more men to defend the land frontiers of Canada and South Africa, as well as its naval stations such as Singapore. Naval blockades of Russia would also be ineffective against the power of the railway, even if Russia could be isolated diplomatically. Mahan had acknowledged this weakness of sea power himself in 1896. Even if Russia had wanted to rely on sea-going traffic, the Declaration of Paris in 1856 made neutral vessels inviolate and there was no question that Russia would make use of foreign vessels to her advantage.

Anglo-Russian differences over Persia were settled in 1907

There had been tension in Persia in the 1890s. Russian territories bordered this Middle Eastern state from Armenia and Central Asia. Against a background of bitter commercial rivalry, spying and gesturing for prestige, Britain and Russia sought to preserve their influence over Persia. The British were concerned that the Russians had gained the upper hand at Teheran, because the Shah's bodyguard included a troop of Cossacks. However, Russia's defeat in the Far East neutralised the threat to Persia and therefore the threat to India. In 1907, the two powers agreed to formalise their areas of influence, and to respect the borders of Afghanistan, in the Anglo-Russian Convention. They agreed that their spheres of influence lay adjacent to their borders, with a 'no-man's land' in between. Britain therefore settled its differences with its two colonial rivals and commentators spoke of a 'Triple Entente'. This was not an alliance. Britain had merely removed old rivalries. Only France and Russia were secretly allied.

The deterioration of relations with Germany

A new naval threat emerged from Germany

Up to 1894, Chancellor Caprivi had maintained good relations with Britain, but when the Kaiser, Wilhelm II, took over diplomacy he allowed feelings of envy to dictate German policy. The Kaiser's policy of *Weltpolitik* (world influence) threatened the idea of 'splendid isolation', because Britain would have to be able to protect its most isolated colonies and outposts from German aggression. This was apparent in a number of incidents. In January 1896, the Kaiser sent a congratulatory note to President Kruger, expressing his approval at the defeat of the British Jameson Raid. Three German ships patrolled Delegoa Bay and the Royal Navy was sent to monitor them. The following year the German Naval Laws increased the size of the German fleet. There was speculation about the need for this, and it appeared that Germany was going to challenge Britain's control of the seas.

Germany also posed an economic threat

The Germans began to court Ottoman (and later, Turkish nationalist) support and launched a project to build the Berlin–Baghdad Railway. This would alter the economic domination of the Middle East by Britain and Russia in Germany's favour. In addition, German goods were being 'dumped' (sold at cheap prices) in South American markets where British goods had been paramount. German steel production was catching up with Britain, and German protectionism had raised hostile tariffs keeping British goods out of Germany and its colonies.

Germany was a military threat to Britain
German weapons were sold to the Boers prior to the South African War (1899–1902) and their Mauser rifles proved devastating against the British army. German volunteers also fought on the Boer side. Kruger was received by the Kaiser when he fled the Transvaal. These events strongly suggested that Germany would support powers hostile to Britain in the future. Germany also possessed one of the most powerful armies in the world. The peacetime strength of her army was just under 700,000 men and it was well equipped with artillery and machine guns.

Germany was unable to settle its differences with Britain
Two attempts to forge closer relations with Germany failed in 1898–99 and, despite a cordial visit by the Kaiser to Britain in 1900, Germany remained committed to the Triple Alliance. Attempts were made, after 1906, to slow down the arms race, but the Kaiser was convinced it had to drive France and Britain apart by the threat of a vast fleet. The Kaiser believed that Germany had to assert itself on the world stage and prove its fitness for world leadership by military and naval strength. In 1908, the Kaiser's comments from an interview with a British friend were printed in the *Daily Telegraph*, with the Kaiser's approval. He described the British as 'mad as March hares' for believing that he had aggressive designs on Britain's Empire, but noted that the German people and his own politicians probably hated the British. These inflammatory comments caused consternation in Germany, and outrage in Britain.

The First Moroccan Crisis, 1905–6, tested the Entente
In 1904, Britain had agreed that France should eventually acquire Morocco, but the Kaiser decided to land at Tangier during a Mediterranean cruise in 1905 to announce that he was in favour of Moroccan independence and called for an international conference on the matter. The Kaiser intended that France would be humiliated and he doubted that Britain would support the French, despite the Entente. In fact, Sir Edward Grey assured the French of Britain's support at the Algerciras Conference, and arranged that the USA would also back the French. Russia, as France's ally, also did so. Germany was only supported by Austria-Hungary. After the conference, secret military talks in 1906 between British and French officers discussed the positioning of the British army in Europe if war ever broke out.

An arms race developed between Britain and Germany
In 1906, the Royal Navy began work on a revolutionary new design of battleship, *H.M.S. Dreadnought*. With a speed of 21 knots and armed with ten 12-inch guns,

she was the most powerful ship of her day and a revolutionary new design. However, so advanced was the ship, that it rendered all others obsolete and this meant that any power copying the Dreadnought class would be able to compete with Britain on level terms. The Liberals, eager to find money for their social reform programme, tried to slow down the construction of ships. In 1906, three ships were ordered, not four. In 1907, this had dropped to two. Tirpitz, the Commander of the German High Seas Fleet, immediately saw an opportunity to surpass Britain and he stepped up construction to three of the new Nassau class (the German equivalent of the Dreadnought). In 1909, McKenna, the First Lord of the Admiralty, asked for six Dreadnoughts to be constructed each year, in order to keep ahead of Germany and maintain Britain's naval strength. The Cabinet was divided, and some wanted just four new ships each year, but a press campaign demanded 'We want eight and we won't wait!'. The government gave way, and construction was increased. In 1914, Britain had 19 at sea, and 13 under construction. Germany had completed 13 but was building a further seven. This competitiveness, and the possibility that Germany could defeat the Royal Navy, led to speculation that the Kaiser might be planning the invasion of Britain. Erskine Childers' novel, *The Riddle in the Sands*, on this subject was highly popular and a spy fever gripped the public imagination.

The Second Moroccan Crisis, 1911
On 1 July 1911, the German gunboat *Panther* was sent to the Moroccan port of Agadir. This aggressive gesture was justified by the German Foreign Minister, Kiderlen Waechter, as the protection of German interests. He alleged that France had broken its agreement of 1906 that Moroccan independence would be respected. In Britain, the German naval action seemed further evidence that Germany planned to assert its naval supremacy in the region. There was even speculation that the Germans would try to annex Agadir for themselves as a naval base, probably as reward from the Moroccans for supporting their independence. Indeed, the Kaiser was trying to convince Muslim leaders across the Middle East that he was in favour of a pan-Islamic revival. A German base, close to Gibraltar and the trade routes through the South Atlantic, was seen as a direct threat to Britain's interests. Lloyd George, in a famous address at the Mansion House on 21 July, warned Germany that Britain would not tolerate this aggression. Haldane, the Minister of War, reinforced Britain's position.

The crisis marked the nadir of Anglo-German relations
The German government regarded the British reaction as warlike, and, in the War Council meeting the following year, one official in the Kaiser's inner circle recorded an atmosphere of *Kriegslustig* (desire for war). Although the Kaiser wanted the 'Great Fight' straight away, Tirpitz urged Wilhelm II to wait a further 18 months so that the German High Seas Fleet could build up its strength. Germany had continued negotiations with the French and eventually, despite

moments of tension in November 1911, settled for 'compensation' in the form of territory in the French Congo. However, relations between Britain and Germany were strained. The War Office and the Admiralty began to co-ordinate their efforts, planning the defence of Britain in the event of war. In 1912, the Royal Navy worked with its French counterpart in reorganising the distribution of fleets. The French concentrated their main effort in the Western Mediterranean. The Royal Navy took up responsibility for the Channel and the North Sea. The implication of this decision was that, if war broke out and Britain did not join France, the northern French coast would be exposed to German attack.

The causes of the First World War

The causes of the First World War can be divided into long-term 'conditions' and short-term 'trigger' factors. Tensions had built up over imperial rivalry, particularly because the Kaiser was fond of making dramatic gestures, like the Kruger Telegram, or making demands for a 'place in the sun'. Suspicion surrounded his fondness for militarism too. The Kaiser often appeared in uniform and surrounded himself with military men. He thought of himself as a skilful commander, but his arrogance invited anger if not ridicule. Related to this was his enthusiasm for the arms race with Britain. He was eager to rival the Royal Navy, and, if possible, defeat it. He wanted to see the German Empire supersede the British one. A series of international crises in Morocco and in the Balkans convinced some of the Great Powers that a military solution was required to end the diplomatic impasse. Yet the 'July Crisis', following the assassination of Franz Ferdinand, the Austrian heir to the throne, by Serbian terrorists on 28 June 1914, was the incident that triggered the war. Serbia called on its ally, Russia, whilst Austria was supported by Germany. Russia, in turn, looked to France for support against Germany.

The alliance system did not cause the war
Nevertheless, it was not the alliance system that caused the war. The alliances simply accelerated the participation of the leading powers. It was the German solution to a war on two fronts that turned a limited conflict into a European war. Germany's aggressive war plans required an invasion of France and her rapid defeat even if she had not officially declared war. This was so that Germany could then turn her outnumbered forces against Russia which would be slower to mobilise. Success depended on speed and the fastest route to envelop Paris involved crossing neutral Belgium. The Kaiser knew that this would involve war with Britain, because it was pledged to protect the Belgian borders. The Kaiser felt that the British could only field a 'contemptible little army' that would have no effect on the great numbers of his own forces as they swept in arc across northern France and Flanders.

Imperialism and the arms race created tension but were not direct causes of the war
Whilst imperial rivalries did exist, they do not mean that Europeans went to war because of them in 1914. In fact, it could be argued that the resolution of these tensions at conferences like the West Africa Conference, the Algerciras Conference and the Franco-German negotiations of 1911, proved that the Great Powers could co-operate successfully. The arms race, and the division of Europe into 'two armed camps', did not simply cause the war, but the sense of fear they generated was significant in affecting the decision-makers. The existence of mass armies which took time to mobilise and leave a country vulnerable in that critical period, or the chance that a battlefleet might be defeated and coasts left unguarded, was on the minds of the European rulers in 1914.

Domestic crises affecting the Great Powers may have contributed to the war
There is some evidence from the historian Hans Ulrich Wehler that Germany's élites went to war to avert a period of unrest or even a revolution. The growth of the Social Democratic Party in Germany, and the widespread popularity of socialist ideas, convinced the Kaiser and his military élite to consider a war in order to reunite the German people with patriotic sentiment. Russia's élites tried to cope with revolutionary groups and saw war as an opportunity to rally the people behind the Tsar, although they were eager to avoid another war unless they were assured of victory. When Austria annexed Bosnia in the Balkans in 1908, Russia's military weakness (after the 1905 defeat) was obvious. Between 1908 and 1914, Russia was arming herself more quickly than any other power. France had itself been divided over the Dreyfus Affair which highlighted the difference between the left and the right wings. The emergence of the radical left also pointed to the idea that France needed some force to bind her together again. Austria-Hungary was troubled by the uncertain loyalty of the southern Slavs, and the threat this posed to an Empire made up of national minorities. In an age of nationalism, it is remarkable perhaps that the Austrian Empire lasted as long as it did. In 1914, the Austrians were eager to crush the Serbian nationalists both within and outside their borders.

The Serbians attracted little sympathy at first
The Balkan Wars (1912–13) concluded with the defeat first of Turkey and then of Bulgaria. In both conflicts, Serbia was victorious. She acquired more territory, and more manpower for her armed forces. She also gained valuable military experience. Having defeated the Ottoman Empire, the Serbians felt emboldened against Austria-Hungary. Serbian nationalists, led by the Chief of Intelligence, organised the assassination of the Austrian heir at Sarajevo on 28 June 1914. The assassination was, in itself, a minor incident. It was by no means inevitable that a European war would result, except that the Serbian government did appear to have had knowledge that the attack would be carried out. When an Austrian ultimatum was delivered, Britain and France urged acceptance of its terms. Serbia did so, agreeing to refer an investigation of conspiratorial activities to

international supervision through the Hague. When Serbia was threatened with war, the British press were uninterested in such a distant part of Europe. One headline announced 'To Hell with Serbia!'

Germany, Austria and Russia appeared to favour war
Russia was determined not to be humiliated again (as she had been in 1908) and was determined to support Serbia against Austria. However, the German General Staff and the Kaiser gave unequivocal support to the Austrian Government, the so-called 'blank cheque', which implied military support against Russia. The Austrians (especially Conrad von Hotzendorff, the Chief of Staff) felt this was the last chance to deal with Serbia. Sir Edward Grey tried to persuade the Kaiser to restrain Austria and called for an international conference. However, once these Great Powers began to mobilise, it was difficult to avert war because there was limited time for diplomacy. There was a calculation that a failure to mobilise might also give their enemies an advantage. The Kaiser ignored Grey because he knew his war plan only catered for an attack on France before Russia, even if France had not declared war.

There was division in the British Cabinet about the coming war
The preservation of peace was one of the most important Liberal principles, but Sir Edward Grey was having little success in this respect in the summer of 1914. There were a number of concerns about the future if Britain did not support France. There was a strong possibility that France would be defeated, which would mean German hegemony in Europe. Germany had already caught up with Britain's industrial production, but the domination of all of Europe's resources would mean the creation of a Wilhelmine superstate and the exclusion of British trade by aggressive tariffs. Britain was also morally obliged to assist France following the secret military and naval talks of 1906 and 1912. Cambon dramatically asked: 'I am waiting to see if the word honour should be struck out of the English language'. It was not until 30 July that the Cabinet considered the question of Belgium, but Grey's failure to convince other powers to remain at peace made such a discussion less important anyway. When Germany attacked Belgium, it rallied the Cabinet. There had been a breach of international law and Britain was directly involved in the preservation of that law. The idea of a 'gallant little Belgium' was an attractive explanation for the British people and it was in the defence of Belgium that Britain declared war on 4 August 1914.

Tutorial

Progress questions
1. What imperial questions caused a deterioration in relations between Britain and Germany?

2. What effect did the German plans for a Berlin–Baghdad railway have on Britain and its traditional rivalry with Russia?

3. What effect did the British rapprochement with France in 1904 have on Germany?

4. What effect did the launching of *H.M.S. Dreadnought* in 1906 have on Britain's naval strength and Germany's maritime ambitions?

5. Why did relations between Britain and Germany deteriorate in 1911–12, and what was done to improve them?

Seminar discussion
What factors compelled Britain to participate in the Great War, and what importance should we attach to them?

Practical assignment
Make a timeline of events that led to the Great War, charting the decay of relations between Germany and Britain.

Study tips
1. Devise a list a reasons for the First World War and assess Britain's part in each of them. Notice how Britain aimed to avert war, but how Germany assumed Britain was already an ally of France.

2. Make sure you are aware of the differences between international tensions and the actual causes of the war. Although imperial rivalries had been important, the European powers were unlikely to risk a war over them even in 1906 and 1912.

3. You will need to be able to explain why Germany was so aggressive between 1895 and 1914. Britain's foreign policy was largely a reaction to Germany's.

10

The Great War, I: 1914–1916

One-minute summary – The First World War, or the Great War as it was known to contemporaries, was the first total war. Although there was a strong public expectation of quick victory, many military men, such as Lord Kitchener knew from the outset that it would be a long war. When the opening battles of 1914 degenerated into trench stalemate on the Western Front, alternatives were sought in the Near East where Britain could 'knock away the props' of Germany by defeating her allies. Although Britain retained her naval supremacy and achieved remarkable successes in Africa, the 'siege warfare' in France and Belgium cost thousands of lives. Gearing up for a total war, the government was forced to abandon its peacetime principles. Provided with more munitions and fresh troops, the army tried to break through on the Somme. Here, valuable lessons were learnt, but at a terrible price.

In this chapter you will learn:

▶ why there was stalemate on the Western Front
▶ how the British army tried to break the stalemate
▶ what alternatives were sought to the Western Front in other theatres
▶ what economic changes were bought about to fight a total war
▶ how Ireland was affected by the war
▶ the importance of the Battle of the Somme.

The Western Front, 1914–15

The British army performed well at Mons and Le Cateau

The BEF (British Expeditionary Force), numbering 100,000 men, was commanded by Sir John French and its task was to 'support and co-operate with the French army'. Its size was its greatest weakness, and, although the British did not know it, the main effort of the German army was to be placed against it. Von Moltke, the German Chief of Staff, aimed to swing his armies through Flanders, across the rivers Meuse and Somme, to envelop Paris. At Mons on 23 August 1914, the BEF demonstrated its firepower was out of all proportion to its size, as it inflicted over 5,000 casualties on the advancing German First Army. German officers complained that the British were all armed with machine guns, but in fact, the marksmanship and rapid fire drills of individual British soldiers was the reality. Riflemen could produce fifteen aimed rounds a minute. Moreover, they had learnt their lessons from South Africa. Their uniforms were designed to blend in with their surroundings and they fought using all available cover. However, to avoid being overwhelmed, it was necessary to fall back in line with their French allies. The fighting withdrawal inevitably cost lives and so at Le Cateau, the Commander of II Corps, Sir Horace Smith Dorrien, decided to give the Germans a 'stopping blow'. The centre of the line easily checked the German attacks, but once again there was a risk of being outflanked. The battle and the extraction cost the BEF 7,200 men, but it created a breathing space. The 'Retreat from Mons' continued after Le Cateau, but without the immediate risk of envelopment which had characterised its first few days. News that the German armies had swung south before reaching Paris seemed to offer the chance of a counter-attack. The French did so, checking the German armies on the Marne. However, the Germans began to dig in along the river Aisne, and, in order to outflank them, it was necessary for the BEF to march north to Ypres.

Lines of trenches extended across Belgium and France as the BEF suffered heavily
Both sides tried to outflank each other in the so-called 'race to the sea', but lines of trenches marked the consolidation of the troops and soon a network extended 500 km from Switzerland to the English Channel. To break the, as yet, thin line, the Germans launched an attack at Ypres against the depleted BEF. On 31 October, the Germans almost broke through, but there were desperate counter-attacks where even support troops (grooms, cooks, transport men) were rushed into the firing line. The London Scottish, the first Territorial battalion in action, defended Messines Ridge alongside the regulars, an indication that the war would require more of its citizens to hold the front. The main German attack was delivered on 11 November, and a gaping hole in the line was plugged by a courageous charge by the Oxford and Buckinghamshire Light Infantry. The BEF suffered heavy casualties: 58,000 died between Mons and First Ypres. The size of a battalion before the fighting was 1,000 men, but after Ypres, the average number of original survivors was 30. Units were reinforced, but the figures give some idea of the scale of sacrifice made by the professional soldiers of the British army. The Germans had also suffered terribly. They called Ypres *Kindermord*: massacre of the innocents.

Attempts to break the stalemate on the Western Front

There was an urgent need for men and munitions
Opinions were divided on the solution to the stalemate which had developed on the Western Front. Churchill and Lloyd George favoured holding on the west, but perhaps attacking Germany's allies elsewhere. Sir John French felt that the primary aim had been the support of the French, and that the war would be decided by the defeat of Germany in the west. However, in the short term, the British army needed more men and it needed munitions. Field Marshal Lord Kitchener, the Secretary of State for War, disapproved of the Territorials ('town clerks' army') and was unfamiliar with the ponderous bureaucratic machinery of

Whitehall, so he launched his own appeal for men to enlist in the New Armies. The response was overwhelming. In just eight weeks, 761,000 men joined up. Some of these new units were drawn almost exclusively from one area or profession, and the close camaraderie gave rise to the title 'Pals Battalions'. The shortage of personnel to give training led to the re-employment of retired officers (called 'dug outs' because they had been dug out of retirement). There was also a shortage of uniforms and weapons. In France, regulars were brought from the Empire to fill the trenches, but they too suffered shortages. There was an urgent need for sandbags, barbed wire, machine guns and, above all, ammunition.

The offensives of 1915 were hamstrung by a lack of ammunition

Sir John French decided to attack at Neuve Chappelle and then to push on to Aubers Ridge whereupon the cavalry would fan out into the country beyond. The first assault on 10 March was successful but it was almost impossible to know what was happening at the front so the attack on Aubers Ridge was delayed. Telephone wires were cut by shell fire. The shell-torn ground also made it difficult to get supplies and ammunition forward, and this greatly assisted the defenders. The Germans capitalised on the delay, which was extended by their own experimental attacks using poison gas at Ypres in April. Gas had proved effective against unprotected troops, but it failed to provide the Germans with any breakthrough. At Aubers Ridge, the Germans built supporting trench lines, constructed concrete pill boxes, increased the depth of their barbed wire and brought up more reserves. When the British attack went in on 8 May, it had only one fifth of the artillery fire of before. There were 11,500 casualties. Sir John French was furious, particularly when he discovered that 22,000 shells had been sent to Gallipoli. In some cases, guns were issued with three rounds per day. Charles Repington reported the news in *The Times* and French challenged his superiors. As the First Sea Lord had just resigned, Asquith decided to form a coalition government. His hesitation and concern for economy was inappropriate for war leadership, but he remained Prime Minister.

The Battle of Loos indicated the problems of the Western Front

Against Sir John French's advice, the French commander, Joffre, and Lord Kitchener demanded an attack to support a French assault at Artois and to support the Russians who had been driven out of Warsaw. The position was a strong one. Amongst the slag heaps of an industrial area, the German army had constructed two belts of defences. They were supported by considerable numbers of reserves and artillery. The numerous towers of the mining operations offered excellent observation posts to direct their guns. The width of the attack on 25 September reduced the intensity of the artillery fire and infantrymen were unable to cross uncut barbed wire. The first use of gas by the British army produced little result, and 2,000 were incapacitated when wind blew the gas back into British trenches. Once again, communication with the leading waves was difficult once the battle had begun. As a result of the battle, Sir John French was sacked and Sir Douglas Haig, who had been critical of the Commander in Chief, was appointed to replace him.

Alternatives to the Western Front: the other theatres of war

The Gallipoli campaign was designed to 'knock away the props'

Turkish ships bombarded the Russian ports in the Black Sea prompting Russia, then France and Britain to declare war on 5 November 1914. However, the Turks closed the Dardanelles to all shipping and Russia was soon dependent on the ice-bound ports of Archangel and Vladivostok for supplies. It was also hoped that Greece and Bulgaria might join the Entente powers against their old enemies, the Turks. Churchill, the First Lord of the Admiralty, aimed to send a flotilla of older vessels to force through the Dardanelles strait and bombard Constantinople. The naval attack was checked by mines laid in the narrow channel on 15 March 1915 so it was clear that landings would be required to support the Royal Navy from the coast. On 25 April, British troops went ashore at Cape Helles but were unable to penetrate the Turkish defences in the hills above them. Despite major attacks on 6–8 May, a stalemate developed. Fresh landings at Anzac Cove (named after the Australian and New Zealand Army Corps that landed there) and Suvla Bay failed to make any headway. In September, fresh German attacks on Serbia demanded the British switch their efforts to Salonika where they could keep open communications. This decision was confirmed when Bulgaria joined the Central Powers in October. In January 1916, the Gallipoli beachheads were abandoned. In 1918, the Salonika force was able to break out of its position and contributed to the defeat of Bulgaria. Nevertheless, Turkey was defeated by operations further south.

The Turks were attacked in the Near East and the Middle East

The Indian army was tasked with the protection of oil supplies at Abadan, at the head of the Persian Gulf. Basra was occupied in November 1914 and General Townshend led an expeditionary force up the Tigris, defeating Turkish forces at Kut el Amara and Ctesiphon in 1915. However, outnumbered, he was forced to retire to Kut which was besieged for five months. The garrison surrendered in April 1916, but most of the 12,000 prisoners of war died in Turkish camps. In 1917, General Maude recaptured Kut and drove on to Baghdad. British operations tied down Turkish troops and successfully protected vital oil supplies. A Turkish attack on the Suez Canal was repulsed in February 1915 and in early 1916, General Murray advanced as far as Gaza. Captain T.E. Lawrence worked alongside the Arabs, who had rebelled against Turkish rule in 1916, and captured the port of Aqaba on the Red Sea. In 1917, General Allenby outflanked Turkish defences at Gaza, and on 9 December, he captured Jerusalem. Although delayed by the need to send troops to France, Allenby defeated the Turkish army at Megiddo in September 1918 and the following month, Turkey sued for peace.

The war extended into Africa and Asia

South African troops launched attacks into German South West Africa and captured it in July 1915, despite having to deal with a Boer uprising in December 1914. Togoland had fallen in August 1914, but Kamerun held out until the close of 1915, mainly because of disease amongst the Imperial troops. In German East Africa, Indian troops were repulsed in November 1914, and the war descended into a series of scattered cross-border attacks. In early 1916, General Smuts (formerly a Boer Commando leader) and South African forces drove the German garrison southwards. British-trained East African and West African forces then relieved Smuts' force, and continued to drive the Germans south before pursuing them into Rhodesia. In the Pacific, Japan seized German territories whilst Australian and New Zealand forces took Samoa and some of the German Pacific islands.

The naval blockade and the Battle of Jutland

Britain's naval supremacy proved vital in securing final victory in the First World War. Despite minor actions in 1914 and 1915, where German surface raiders were tracked down and sunk, the only major engagement of the war was the Battle of Jutland in January 1916. Although the Royal Navy lost more vessels, the German High Seas Fleet limped back to port and never reappeared. This enabled Britain to maintain a blockade of German North Sea ports and protect the lifeline to Russia. The German response was to concentrate on U-boat (submarine) warfare. There was a steady increase in the numbers of British merchant ships being sunk. In April 1917, the worst month of the war, Britain lost 869,000 tons of shipping (373 ships). It was estimated that Britain had barely six weeks' supply of food left in the summer of 1917. Defeating U-boats was difficult. In the 142 engagements between destroyers and German submarines, only seven U-boats had been sunk. The temptation to starve Britain through the total destruction of all merchant ships compelled Germany to announce unrestricted U-boat warfare in January 1917. With evidence of the sinking of the *Lusitania* in 1915, where 12,000 had died (including 128 Americans), the decision brought the USA into the war.

The British economy and the war

The war effort was well supported by the public

The British people believed that the war was a righteous one. Germany had violated the borders of a neutral country and invaded France. Germany occupied French and Belgian soil, and exploited the industry it found there for its own war effort. Germany was an autocracy and the Kaiser's plans were militaristic and acquisitive. News also filtered back to Britain through refugees, that the German army treated Belgian and French civilians with high-handedness. In 1915, the sinking of the passenger ship *Lusitania* seemed to indicate that Germany would not respect the protection of non-combatants in war, a fact reinforced by the first Zeppelin raids. Edith Cavell, a British nurse, had been captured in 1915 and was shot, accused of spying, whilst the use of poison gas (a breach of the Hague Protocol of 1908) was regarded as yet more evidence of German 'frightfulness'. Patriotism was a strong motivation for enlisting, but it also sustained those at home. However, once in the trenches, soldiers tended to fight for their immediate friends, units and leaders.

The Defence of the Realm Act (DORA) represented the first of the wartime measures

The first DORA of 8 August 1914, gave special powers to the Cabinet. It did not have to wait for the approval of Parliament, and could impose measures via the Admiralty and the Army Council necessary for the defence of the United Kingdom. This enabled the government to impose censorship to protect public morale, and intern anyone suspected of hostile sympathies. After the initial flood of volunteers, a scheme was designed in October 1915 to enable men to attest to their willingness to serve when the time came. The huge demand for manpower outstripped the supply of volunteers and conscription on all unmarried men between 18 and 41 was imposed. At first, in the urgency of the first weeks of the war, there had been little concern about who had volunteered, but it became apparent that some men who had enlisted were needed at home in factories, mines and transport systems. 'Reserved occupations' were identified. In May 1916, all men were conscripted or directed in labour. Conscription was a death blow to liberalism. It ran contrary to the concept of individual liberty and starkly demonstrated state direction.

Britain geared itself for total war

From the outset, Britain faced some shortages, but they were limited. The government made bulk purchases of wheat and sugar which were scarce after U-boat attacks, and aimed to safeguard the supply of Indian jute (for sandbags) and Russian flax (for tent canvas). However, prices did increase by 59% between July 1914 and June 1916. This wartime inflation was to be expected, but it hit the poorest the hardest. In 1916, there was some local rationing initiatives, but no national scheme until 1918. The shell shortage had caused the biggest concern. With the formation of the Coalition Cabinet in 1915, Asquith appointed Lloyd George to be the Minister of Munitions. In January 1915, the army received its first batch of Stokes' Trench Mortars thanks to Lloyd George's efforts. Despite Kitchener's scepticism, Lloyd George also ordered 40 of Major Swinton's 'landships' under the codename of 'tanks'. The Munitions of War Act brought munitions and armaments factories under government control and banned strikes, lock-outs and drunkenness. The ministry Lloyd George created was unorthodox. Housed in a hotel outside Parliament, it was staffed with business-men of 'push and go', rather than civil servants. Despite the claim that it produced startling results, its first consignment of shells did not reach the front until October

1915 and the War Office had already produced a nineteen-fold increase in ammunition in the first six months of the war.

Trade unions increased their power during the war

It was obvious that Britain would not be able to sustain a strike wave like 1910–13 and win the war at the same time, so Asquith was eager to placate the unions and gain their support. The shortage of manpower added to the bargaining power of the TUC. Under the terms of the Treasury Agreement in March 1915, unions in war work would forego the right to strike and would abandon restrictive trade practices in return for limitations to private profits and the restoration of pre-war conditions when the war was over. Trade unions leaders also approved the Munitions of War Act. The new accommodation was confirmed when Henderson, and later G.N. Barnes, J. Clynes and J. Hodge joined the Cabinet. However, some union members were angry that the strike weapon had been abandoned so readily. Locally elected members even replaced the official TUC candidates. On 'red' Clydeside, there were angry protests and a hostile reception for Lloyd George in Glasgow in December 1915 led to the arrest of the union ringleaders. Industrial disputes actually increased during the war, from 532 in 1915 to 1,165 in 1918. Eight separate commissions found that grievances included the cost of living, war profiteering, conscription, administrative incompetence, and dilution of labour (replacing skilled men with unskilled labour, male or female).

Ireland and the Great War

Irish loyalties were divided by the outbreak of war

When the Great War broke out, the Ulster Volunteers formed the Ulster Division of the British army as a mark of loyalty. They fought with distinction throughout the Great War and suffered particularly heavy losses at the battle of the Somme in 1916. The Irish Volunteers also joined the British army. Redmond told them that they were fighting for Catholics in Belgium, but large numbers were joining up anyway. Some felt that it was their duty since they were still part of the United Kingdom, others looked for adventure. However, a handful of extremists believed that 'England's difficulty was Ireland's opportunity'. The Irish Volunteers therefore split. The name Irish Volunteers was retained by those who took the extreme line, whilst Redmond's followers were retitled the National Volunteers.

The idea of national sacrifice has had a long legacy

It was not long before the Irish Volunteers also split. A small, hard-line group called the IRB (Irish Republican Brotherhood) divorced themselves from the Volunteers and began to plan a rebellion against British rule. The leaders were Padraic Pearse (a utopian, romantic schoolteacher), James Connolly (socialist and Irish Nationalist) and Eamon de Valera (born in New York and a schoolteacher). The IRB was supported by Sir Roger Casement, a disaffected former British consular official. Pearse called for a 'violent gesture', even a sacrifice, with success necessarily being essential. This tragic attitude reflected the view of the time; the war was thought to be a 'cleansing' process for old problems, and only a great blood sacrifice was appropriate when thousands were dying in the trenches. Connolly was in favour of preparation for a rising, but the training was still inadequate, which has lent an air of heroic failure to the myths that came later. Nevertheless, there was an ominous sense that violence for its own sake was the purpose of the rebellion. According to Professor George Boyce, the blood sacrifice of these nationalists has persuaded generations of nationalists to see any compromise as a 'sell out' to the ideals of these men. For loyalists, the heroic sacrifice of Ulstermen on the Somme, dying for their country and their cause, has given a similar sense of commitment for their successors ever since.

The Easter Rising 1916: preparations
There were a number of problems in the preparation of the Rising. It was, to some extent, dependent on the arrival of German arms. The Royal Navy intercepted the German ship, the *Aud* (which was scuttled), leaving the rebels with no other means of resistance. McNeill, the Chief of Staff for the IRB, was deliberately misled by his colleagues. McNeill had wanted to delay the Rising, but the other conspirators passed him a letter that showed the British were about to capture and disarm the volunteers which made action imperative. The letter was a forgery. When he discovered this, he cancelled the orders for a Rising. Roger Casement tried to recruit Irish Prisoners of War in Germany for the Rising. The prisoners were uninterested. Casement was landed in Ireland by a German submarine hoping to halt the Rising because of his failure to enlist men, but he was captured on the beach. The IRB Council decided to delay the Rising until Easter Monday, but with so few men or resources they would only be able to seize the centre of Dublin. This was supposed to act as a spark to a general uprising by the people.

The course of the Easter Rising
The Rising itself began as 1,600 IRB volunteers seized the General Post Office in Dublin as its headquarters. Twelve thousand British troops, supported by artillery and the gunboat *Helga* engaged the IRB in street fighting. By Sunday 30 April, when Pearse and Connolly ordered the surrender, 450 had died and 2614 were wounded, many of whom were civilians. (Included in these figures were 116 British soldiers killed and 368 wounded.) Far from signalling a general Rising, Dubliners were appalled at the damage and regarded the Rising as a futile gesture.

The aftermath of the Rising changed opinion in Ireland
To the British, already under pressure in France, the action of the IRB was nothing short of treachery. General Maxwell was determined to prevent more disturbances. He angered local opinion by arresting 3,430 men and 79 women and interrogating them. Some were released, but 1841 were interned in England. Of

the ringleaders, 15 were executed. Connolly, who had been wounded in the fighting, was strapped to a chair and shot. De Valera was only saved by an appeal to the US Consulate on the grounds that he was half American. The rising was a squalid episode, but the British response, although legal in wartime, turned the Irish public against them. General Maxwell continued to serve as the commander in Ireland until 1918, when Lord French took over, but Augustine Birrell (the Chief Secretary), who had ignored the existence of the IRB between 1914 and 1916, resigned. Redmond's Nationalist supporters dwindled, replaced by the more extreme Sinn Fein, and De Valera was released from gaol in July 1917 whereupon he won the East Clare seat as an anti-British candidate.

The government tried to encourage compromise

In May 1916, Lloyd George tried to bring Carson and Redmond together. He promised Redmond that Ulster's exclusion from a united Ireland would be temporary. To Carson, he suggested that exclusion would be permanent. Clearly Lloyd George was hoping for a compromise in the short term, and banking on a softening of sectarian antagonism in the longer term. However, the Conservative members of the Cabinet refused to accept that Ulster might be cut off and the talks broke down. In July 1917, the Irish Convention was set up, but Sinn Fein refused to join. Ulstermen argued that they would not, indeed they could not, make concessions. The Convention lasted until July 1918.

The Battle of the Somme

There are criticisms of Haig's plans

The Somme is perhaps the best known and most remembered of all the battles of the First World War. This is largely because of the high casualties that were sustained on the first day of the battle; 57,000 were killed and wounded, which the most costly day in the history of the British army. The Somme is also synonymous with the blunders of the war. However, the battle looks quite different when it is viewed in context.

Haig chose the Somme for a grand set-piece offensive. The argument runs that the site was poorly chosen because the Germans had excellent views of the British as they attacked uphill from the Ancre Valley. The second accusation is that Haig's troops were too inexperienced compared with the German soldiers; Haig perhaps thought that he could pit the enthusiasm of the British volunteer civilians against the machine guns of the German army. The third criticism was about his use of artillery. A massive bombardment was supposed to smash the German trenches and barbed wire. Then, at the appointed hour, waves of British soldiers would get up out of their trenches and walk forward, carrying 60lbs of equipment, to occupy the German trenches.

Historians are divided about Haig's performance
In the event, when the British attacked, in many places they were cut down by German machine guns and artillery. Ever since, the enormous casualty figures have been put down to the incompetence of the generals. Thanks to *The Donkeys* (1963) by Alan Clark (a reference to the comment alleged to have been made by the German commander Ludendorff, that British soldiers were 'lions led by donkeys'), Gerard de Groot's highly critical biography of Haig and John Laffin's often inaccurate *British Butchers and Bunglers of World War One* (1998), the impression given is that the generals were incapable of any tactical imagination. Nevertheless, some military historians have taken a different view. John Terraine demonstrated that Haig's stoicism reflected the Field Marshal's view that the Western Front was one, long continuous engagement requiring the full mobilisation of national resources and some tough decisions. Keith Simpson listed the mitigating factors as: pre-war inexperience of total war, lack of preparation, the problem of adapting to new technology, the strength of the German army, restraints imposed by the coalition partners (France and Russia) and political interference. Paddy Griffith believed that the army's experiences were cumulative and contrasted the inexperience of the early years with the successes and scientific application of artillery in 1917–18.

Britain had to support France and Russia in 1916
The painful truth was that Britain was obliged to launch an offensive, and Haig insisted that it be planned carefully. The Germans occupied a large slice of Belgium and France, and would not negotiate while it was still strong. Russia was under pressure in the east and France was enduring a massive and costly offensive at Verdun to the south. General Joffre practically begged Haig to launch an attack to divert the Germans from Verdun. Haig was reluctant. The professional soldiers in the British army were few in number, and the volunteers of 'Kitchener's Army' were as yet untried in battle. Haig's first choice for a British offensive was Ypres because it was near the ports (making re-supply easier) and an attack here would try to capture the cluster of German railheads, and that would make the continued occupation of the north untenable for them. However, there was an alternative to the muddy and low lying fields of Flanders. The Somme uplands were chalk where well drained and drier conditions prevailed, especially in summer. The Somme was also the junction of the French and British armies so that a joint attack here, along a 30-mile front, would double its effect on the Germans.

Haig had learnt valuable lessons from 1914 and 1915
Valuable lessons had also been learnt from the fighting of 1914 and 1915 which could be applied here. Artillery fire was going to be delivered in a scientific way. Instead of a random bombardment there would be two phases. A preparatory bombardment would pulverise trenches, wire and strongpoints and demoralise the enemy. On the day of the attack, a creeping barrage would be applied; shells

falling just in front of the advancing troops and lifted and advanced every few minutes. To add to the effect, mine shafts would be dug so that explosives could be detonated underneath the German positions just before the infantry went in. As soldiers trained for the attack, there was a growing sense of optimism. It was felt that it might even be possible to break through the German lines after a day or two. This would enable the cavalry to pour through and pursue the Germans, disrupting their rear areas, perhaps even initiating a general collapse of the Kaiser's army.

The offensive required huge preparations
The British army had never before attempted an attack on this scale. Half a million men were involved. The logistics to support it were staggering. Thousands of shells, guns, cartridges, explosives and guns were required. The army had to be fed, clothed, shod and equipped. Horses, fodder, water, barbed wire, stretchers, nurses, saddlery, workshops, communications wire, nails and a million other things were needed, and with the French under pressure at Verdun, time was short. The artillery firestorm began on 24 June and lasted a week. It was the largest artillery bombardment of the war to that date. The soldiers each carried a rifle, bayonet, 220 rounds of ammunition, gas helmet, wound dressing, two hand grenades, flares, a spade, greatcoat, haversack and two empty sandbags. Some also carried reels of barbed wire, pickets, mortar bombs, signalling equipment, or a Lewis gun and ammunition belts. With these loads, it was hard to make progress over broken ground.

The battle was costly
Prior to the attack, captured German soldiers produced mixed reports; some were demoralised by the shelling, others were unaffected. Behind the front-line trenches were a warren of dugouts and galleries extending back into the hills. Sheltering from the bombardment, the German troops emerged as soon as the shelling lifted and poured fire into the advance. Casualties were high in many units. The 800-strong 16th Middlesex Regiment (the Public Schools Battalion made up of students and staff) was in the first wave at 07.30. At 07.45 they fell back to their start line; 22 officers and 500 men were casualties. However, the 36th Ulster Division captured its first-day objectives, only to be forced back again by German counter-attacks. Some key villages were captured, such as Mametz, and others fell a few days later. Thiepval, the centre of a series of German strongpoints wasn't captured until September. Certain woods, such as Delville or High Wood, became the scene of intense struggles.

There was a continuing search for solutions amidst a grim struggle
On 15 September, the first tanks were used and despite the fact they were few in number, they were a remarkable success. Mechanical unreliability and vulnerability to artillery fire were their greatest weaknesses, but they were the greatest technical innovation of the war. New types of poison gas were tried out too.

However, the refinement in the use of artillery was becoming apparent and it was clear that gunfire dominated. Nevertheless, bad weather, combined with the cratered soil, rendered the battlefield impassable and the offensive was halted in November. The Somme had not produced a breakthrough as expected and had developed into a battle of attrition. Although the British army suffered 400,000 killed, wounded and missing, the Germans losses are estimated to have been 600,000 (the French lost 200,000). A German officer described the Somme as 'the muddy grave of the German army'. Although British soldiers endured terrible conditions and suffered heavy losses, there was still a grim determination to win.

Tutorial

Progress questions
1. What was the achievement of the small BEF in 1914?

2. What methods did Britain try to use to break the deadlock of the Western Front?

3. What effect did the war have on Ireland?

4. Why was the Liberal government reluctant to impose state control during the war?

Seminar discussion
Were the Great War generals incompetent?

Practical assignment
Make a list of all the measures Britain was forced to consider to wage a total war. What obstacles did the army face in trying to win the war? Consider how the government and the generals dealt with these problems.

Study tips
1. It is easy to jump to conclusions about the leadership of the British war effort. Instead of condemnation, try to account for their limitations and the obstacles they faced.

2. Try to find out more about your local community and the Great War. How were local people affected?

3. It is important to know how Britain organised itself and fought the war in order to understand the political leadership struggle that was to follow in 1916.

11

The Great War, II: 1916–1918

One-minute summary – The years 1917 and 1918 were marked by the maturation of a fully operational war economy, and the perfection of tactics based on the battles of 1914–1916. The soldiers and their commanders had more experience and there was a better appreciation of how artillery should be used. The replacement of Asquith as war leader brought a fresh impetus to government. Lloyd George's energy was ideally suited to the crisis. However, the German army had also developed new tactics of defence which, along with atrocious and unseasonable weather brought the 1917 Ypres offensive to a standstill. The French army began to crack up after the battle of Verdun, putting more emphasis on the British war effort. When Russia collapsed in 1918, German troops arrived on the Western Front to resume the attack. Critically short of manpower, Haig and the British troops stemmed the tide as best they could. In the summer of 1918, American reinforcements arrived to assist in a gigantic counter-offensive. By the autumn, the British army had returned to mobile warfare. These attacks in France, and the Royal Navy's blockade caused Germany to sue for peace in November 1918.

In this chapter you will learn:

▶ how Asquith was replaced by Lloyd George as war leader
▶ how the army tried to find solutions to the stalemate in 1917
▶ the methods by which Britain achieved victory in 1918
▶ how the Great War left an important legacy for the British people.

War leadership

Asquith was replaced by Lloyd George

According to A.J.P. Taylor, 'Asquith was as solid as a rock, but like a rock, incapable of movement'. His 'wait and see' approach, which was manifest in endless delays of Cabinet decisions, was contrasted with Lloyd George's dynamism at the Munitions Ministry. The *Daily Mail* described Lloyd George's motto as 'Do it now'. Asquith had been reluctant to intervene in the shell shortage because it would affect private property and he seemed reluctant to co-operate with the French government at a time when close co-ordination was essential. In 1916, Kitchener was killed at sea and Lloyd George took over as Minister of War. After the huge losses on the Somme, Conservatives in the Coalition Cabinet threatened to resign, but Lloyd George knew they would support him. When Asquith resigned, expecting to be reinstated by his colleagues, Lloyd George replaced him. K. Morgan described the new leader's style: 'Lloyd George's war premiership was without parallel in British history. No previous Prime Minister had ever exercised power in so sweeping and domineering a manner'. Although his appointment greatly aided the war effort, Lloyd George had split the Liberal Party and he was blamed for its subsequent demise by Asquith and Herbert Samuel. Churchill blamed Asquith: 'His resignation was a manoeuvre to rout his critics. Instead he gathered more of them like an ageing heavyweight who has been knocked out by a younger, more agile opponent'.

Lloyd George's measures were far-reaching
Lloyd George established a smaller, five-man War Cabinet, made up of Lord Milner, George Curzon, Bonar Law, Henderson and himself. He also established a Cabinet Secretariat to co-ordinate all government departments under the leadership of Sir Maurice Hankey. He filled ministries with non-government experts, such as Joseph Maclay (a shipowner) in charge of shipping and the newspaper magnate, Lord Beaverbrook, in charge of propaganda. Lloyd George also set up a private secretariat (nicknamed 'The Garden Suburb') of advisors which included Waldorf Astor, the owner of the *Observer* newspaper. He directed that food production be increased, and under Sir George Prothero, an additional 3 million acres was cultivated. Wheat production increased by 1 million tons, potatoes by 1.5 million tons. The war saved British agriculture and reversed the long decline which had affected it so severely from 1870. A minimum wage was finally granted to agricultural workers. Rationing was introduced, first for sugar, and later for other products. Bread wasn't rationed and prices on this staple crop were kept down by a subsidy. At sea, Maclay requisitioned almost all private merchant ships for war use. The Admiralty was slow to adopt convoys to protect merchant shipping, because it was thought the number of ships to protect was too vast and the number of protection vessels too few, but experiments in April 1917 proved a success. Lloyd George had urged that convoys be established earlier, and later claimed they were his idea.

The campaigns of 1917

The burden of the Western Front shifted towards the British army
Nivelle's offensive on the Aisne in April 1917 resulted such heavy casualties that it led to mutinies in the French army. Coming on the back of revolutionary unrest in Russia, it was imperative that the British relieve pressure on the other Entente powers. Already at Arras, the British and imperial forces had secured the vital Vimy Ridge. However, subsequent attacks were foiled by the depth of the German positions, for belts of wire, trenches and emplacements succeeded each other behind the front line.

Messines Ridge was a success
General Sir Herbert ('Daddy') Plumer was the commander of 2nd Army tasked

with capturing the Messines Ridge. Securing this high ground would be the prelude to a subsequent attack on the Menin-Broodseinde Ridge. Once taken, the British army would be within striking distance of the main rail junction of Menin from which the Germans were supplying and reinforcing the entire northern front. Plumer's preparations were meticulous. Tunnels were dug under the German front line for explosives to be laid, light railways brought up ammunition in vast quantities, and 2,266 guns fired 3.5 million shells into the German positions. On 7 June, 19 mines were detonated and the British attack captured three lines of German trenches and with them, the entire ridge. The success illustrated what had been learned from the Somme. New fuses enabled artillery to destroy wire, the British infantry were better trained, the Royal Artillery dominated the battlefield and infantry–artillery co-ordination had been perfected. However, there were still heavy casualties; 25,000 had fallen in the battle.

The Third Battle of Ypres (Passchendaele) was a pyrrhic victory
The chief difficulty with the second phase of the operations around Ypres was that the low lying and marshy ground had been smashed by years of shelling. Added to this was the appalling weather that dogged the attack almost from the start. Some sectors became impassable swamps and trenches filled with water. The infantry continued to attack, but often found it impossible to hold on to ground against German counter-attacks. Tanks foundered in the mud. Wounded men were drowned in shellholes. Even some of the concrete emplacements slid into the slough, trapping those inside. This battle, more than any other, inspired comments on war's futility from those that endured it. The conditions were not unfamiliar to the soldiers, but the heavy casualties, gas attacks, shelling and exhausting trial of moving in the quagmire of the Ypres Salient marked the battle out as particularly distinct. Estimates of the casualties by the end of the offensive in November vary, but are thought to be in the region of 260,000. The ridges were captured, but the casualty figures suggest that the price was too high to call it a success. The consolation was that the German army had suffered just as heavily and Ludendorff, the German Commander in Chief, doubted whether the Kaiser's forces could take another blow like Third Ypres.

Future use of tanks was assured by success at Cambrai
The sign of things to come was the remarkable success at Cambrai. Initially conceived of as a raid, massed tank formations captured German lines to a depth of eight miles. A shortage of reserves meant that the ground could not be held for long, but it had proved the worth of the tank. By 1918, British tanks had become far more reliable, and a new light version was being developed.

The victory of 1918

The German spring offensive was overwhelming
Having finally defeated Russia in March 1918, the German army swung its main effort at the British on the Somme. A series of sledgehammer blows drove the Third and Fifth Armies back, but Haig managed to hold the line. Despite criticism from Lloyd George, Haig also held back his reserves until it was clear where the attacks would fall. Unable to break though on the Somme, the Germans tried to break the Second Army at Ypres. Subsequent attacks were made against the French. Lloyd George decided to by-pass Haig by suggesting that the Frenchman Marshal Foch become the supreme allied commander to co-ordinate the defence of the Western Front. Foch was duly appointed, but while Haig maintained a dignified silence about his Prime Minister, Lloyd George broadcast his views that Haig was a 'military Moloch' and that the Somme had been a 'disastrous failure'.

The conscription question caused attitudes to harden in Ireland
Britain's manpower shortage had reached a critical point by 1918. Despite the thousands who had volunteered from the Empire, Britain was faced with the prospect of calling up married men over 45. Ireland had been exempted from conscription in light of the rising, but the prospect of young Catholics going free whilst older married men in Britain were compelled to join up, could no longer be tolerated. Lloyd George wanted to offer Home Rule in return, but there still had been no decision on Ulster, so both conscription and Home Rule were shelved. However, the very rumour that conscription was about to be imposed on Ireland caused the Irish Nationalists to withdraw from the House of Commons. Roman Catholic bishops began to preach against conscription too. Concerns about the security situation in Ireland forced the British to increase the garrison there to 87,500: completely the opposite effect that was desired.

The British army was desperately short of men
Lord French, the Lord Lieutenant of Ireland, decided to arrest the Sinn Fein leaders who were agitating against Britain in May 1918. In France, the British army was enduring the strongest attack of the German army ever mounted. The situation was becoming critical. To avoid another Irish rebellion, 73 Irish Nationalists were deported to England, including De Valera, Arthur Griffith, and William Cosgrave; the latter on suspicion of contacting Germany. This suppression added fuel to Nationalist propaganda, but the British took the threat seriously. The number of battalions in British brigades was reduced from four to three, but there was no disguising the shortage of troops. With years of emphasis on attack, rear areas were ill-prepared to withstand the German attacks. However, the trickle of American troops was becoming a steady stream by early 1918. At first there were too few of these enthusiastic, but inexperienced troops to be used effectively as an independent command, but their presence released

British and French troops from reserves. With these additional men, the German March offensive was checked and then thrown back.

Mobile war returned in the '100 days' campaign from Amiens

Rawlinson, the commander of 4th Army (combining British, Canadian and Anzac troops), maximised the use of tanks, machine guns and artillery co-ordination to achieve considerable success near Amiens. Aircraft dominated the skies, and a rolling barrage in front of the advancing troops repeated the success of 4th Army over several days. On the 8th August, eight miles were captured, and Ludendorff knew that the end was coming. He called it 'the black day of the German army'. The advance continued and the German Hindenburg Line, a strongly fortified system, was broken in September. The Germans continued to fight, but they were pressed back towards their own borders.

The effects of blockade ensured the final collapse of the German war effort

Shortages in Germany caused by the Royal Navy's blockade had reached crisis levels in many cities and food riots were an indication that the war effort could no longer be sustained. There was growing war weariness amongst the troops too. The news from the Western Front led to the collapse of the military government and the Kaiser abdicated. As Plumer cleared the Belgian coast and the British army advanced towards Germany, an Armistice was declared on 11 November 1918.

Interpretations of the First World War

Casualties were an important legacy but not the determinant of victory

The '100 days' and the German capitulation in November 1918 indicate that Britain had won the Great War, but after the war, the scale of the losses gave rise to a determination never to go to war again. Three-quarters of a million British and Empire soldiers, sailors and airmen died on the Western Front. Britain itself lost a total of 650,000 with 1.6 million permanently disabled. For a long time, it was thought that the 'flower' of British youth had perished: the best, brightest and fittest. This was probably because the junior officer corps, drawn from the educated middle classes and the aristocracy, had suffered proportionally higher casualties. However, the terrible losses amongst the Pals Battalions on the Somme devastated small communities. Thousands of families lost at least one family member. Death did not respect rank or status; Asquith lost his son, Bonar Law lost two. Yet Britain would have suffered far worse consequences if, as almost occurred in March-April 1918, the Germans had won. There was little sympathy for the Germans in 1918. An army of occupation stood on the Rhine and the British people demanded that Germany pay for the damage and sorrow it had inflicted on the rest of the world.

> **Casualties**
> 600,000 British men were killed and 1.6 million were wounded.
>
> **Mobilisation**
> 5.7 million men were mobilised during the war.
>
> **Politics**
> The Conservatives (with Lloyd George as leader) dominated the interwar years.
> Labour emerged as the leading opposition party and formed two governments (1924, 1929–31) but was wracked by division in the 1930s.
> The Liberals were relegated to third place.
> Women over 30 were able to vote.
> All men, regardless of property, were able to vote.

Fig. 6. The impact of the Great War on Britain.

Tutorial

Progress questions

1. What measures did Lloyd George implement in the economy during the war?

2. Why was Plumer's attack at Messines Ridge in 1917 a success?

3. What went wrong in the attack at Third Ypres?

4. Why did Britain avoid conscription in Ireland in 1918?

5. By what methods did Britain achieve final victory in 1918?

Seminar discussion

What was different about Britain's war effort, at home and overseas, in 1914–15 and 1918?

Practical assignment

Assess the relative importance of the war at sea, wartime controls at home and battlefield tactics in producing the victory of 1918.

Study tips

1. Note how Asquith failed to appreciate the full implications of total war, whereas Lloyd George dispensed with normal procedures for the sake of urgency.

2. Note that most military historians do not condemn the British generals; historians should try to appreciate the problems that contemporaries faced.

3. The Empire was drawn into the war, making it a global conflict before the USA declared war in 1917. This fact should be used to fully evaluate the purpose of the Empire for contemporaries in this period.

12

Conclusions

One-minute summary – The period 1870–1918 was the birth of modern Britain. There was a greater degree of democracy after the 1867 Reform Act and the Third Reform Act (1884), but, by 1918, there was an irresistible move towards universal manhood suffrage. The war brought other changes. Where the suffragettes had failed to further the enfranchisement of women, the contribution of British women to the war effort succeeded in obtaining the vote for women over 30 in 1918. The logic of representation at local government level and the demonstration of loyalty and responsibility made it possible for women over 30 to vote after the war. Despite the fact that 'war work' had been so important, there was little permanent change to the employment profile of the sexes. Although there was greater democratisation, ironically it was the Liberal Party that suffered, not the Conservatives. A split during the ultimate national crisis hurled the Liberals into the political wilderness, and they never recovered. The war had been a test of the country. Despite concerns about isolation, relative decline, an over-extended Empire and social conflict before 1914, the British people rose to the challenge. The cost was great, but the victory of 1918 was a fitting testimony to the men and women of that era.

In this chapter you will learn:

▶ that there was a greater democratisation of the State
▶ that there were still many continuities in British history
▶ how British society changed.

The democratisation of the State

In 1870, Britain's political élite was made up almost entirely of the aristocracy. The middle classes and the gentry were the natural leaders of industry, commerce and politics because of their education, wealth and influence. This situation itself had a long heritage, stretching back into British history. However, by 1918, Britain's industry was under the direction of the state, many private owners had been suspended from their businesses, and trade unions exercised a stronger voice. Moreover, there was now an educated and literate public. Local government structures, upon which men and women voted, were well established. Serving in the Cabinet were both aristocrats, middle-class and working-class men. Lloyd George himself epitomised the progress that was possible; from rural Wales to the nation's Prime Minister. However, some of these changes were due to the special circumstances of the war. Britain was fighting for its life. Total war measures were required, but there was always an expectation that they would last only for 'the duration'. Indeed, there was a strong conviction that the degree of state ownership exercised during the war was neither desirable nor workable in peacetime.

Continuities in British history

Britain was still drawn into European affairs
Although Britain had tried hard to avoid obligations in Europe in the 1890s, the Great War and its aftermath denied her that luxury. In fact, Britain had always acknowledged that it had a role to play and its interests were inextricably linked to events on the continent. In the 1870s, Britain had intervened in the Eastern Mediterranean to safeguard its trading arteries. Its imperial interests frequently demanded negotiations with other powers to avoid misunderstanding and conflict throughout the 1880s and 1890s. Britain tried hard to maintain the unfettered circulation of trade by avoiding tariffs. It viewed with foreboding the establishment of exclusive spheres of influence around the world by other powers, but, reluctantly perhaps, it also participated.

The British Empire had proved its value as a resource
Thousands of troops had been drawn from the Empire to fight in Britain's colonial wars, policing a system designed to benefit the mother country, but also her subjects. The mutual benefit of imperialism was not always apparent or appreciated. There were plenty of examples where military intervention had been necessary, but the remarkable achievement of the Empire was its ability to command the loyalty of so many of its subjects. The men who fought for Britain provided essential manpower at a critical moment in its history. Economically, the Empire turned Britain into the hub of a global trading system and the world's leading financial centre. There it would have remained for many years had it not been for the war. The war also encouraged nationalist protesters to organise and demand change.

Liberalism was eclipsed
One of the casualties of the war was undoubtedly the Liberal Party. Split by the leadership dispute of 1916, there were already fissures in its surface. The trade unions on the one hand, the aspirations of the working classes on the other (which, of course, frequently overlapped), had witnessed the merits of state ownership. They had seen also the system tested by war. The fairer distribution of food, of profits, and of ownership made Liberal ideas of maintaining private property, and the liberty of the individual redundant for those on the left. Yet this should not be exaggerated. After the war, the Conservatives, not Labour (although Labour and the Liberals had representatives in the 1918 government), held the majority of seats in parliament and dominated the coalition government. Nor was this just another 'khaki election' since Conservatives were returned to government several

times in the inter-war years. Nevertheless, many voted again for the energetic 'man who had won the war': Lloyd George. Compared with the sobriety of Gladstone, Lloyd George seemed to have more in common with the flamboyance and wit of Disraeli. Yet there was a passion in Gladstone's moral crusades, which Lloyd George also brought to his own campaigns.

Conservativism had proved itself a 'popular' force

Despite the pessimism of Salisbury, or Lansdowne fighting his rearguard actions in the House of Lords, the Conservatives had championed popular politics just as much as the Liberals. Disraeli's 1867 Reform Act was revolutionary, Randolph Churchill revived the mantle of Tory Democracy, and the Conservatives were the party of patriotism and Empire, which were forces that could galvanise more people than the churches. Andrew Bonar Law had shown solidarity with the Ulstermen in 1912 too; a paradox where the party that aimed to preserve order and the constitution could contemplate support for the embattled minority who denied the law. It is a curious fact that their nickname, 'Tory', means 'Irish bandit'.

Changes in British society

Provision for the poor had improved

Compared with the indifference of the mid-nineteenth century, by 1918 steps had been taken to tackle poverty. There was still a long way to go before the conditions would be alleviated in both town and country. In parts of Britain, such as Glasgow or the East End of London, there was little visible change between 1900 and 1939. However, there was an education system, health care and some protection at work. After the First World War, there was great optimism that things would continue to improve.

The position of women was not significantly altered

Women's participation in the war effort was considerable. They had taken up vacancies left by men in farms, transport, police, quarries, and foundries. Thirty thousand women worked at Woolwich arsenal alone by 1917, as munitions work increased in scale. However, a 1921 census revealed that, after the war, these women had lost their jobs. In fact, fewer women were employed outside of the home in the 1920s than in 1911. What had changed was the attitude to female suffrage. Women over 30 got the vote in 1918.

There was a greater understanding of how others lived

The First World War was a levelling experience for the troops. Soldiers and officers from different backgrounds were forced to share the same dangers, and often the same dugouts. This brought a new appreciation between men that would have, ordinarily, not met in peacetime. Some working-class men enjoyed the responsibility of command, some middle-class men learnt to respect the gallantry and fortitude of those lower down the social scale. Regions were also brought together. Liverpuddlians, Cockneys, Glaswegians and West Countrymen were thrown together by the war. Mass communications, trains, and telephones, also contributed to this process of course. There was also greater contact with troops from the Empire. The products of the colonies had long been familiar to the British consumer, but there was some new interaction with Diggers, Kiwis and Springboks. The class system survived in Britain, and was not radically different in 1918 from 1900, but there was a greater understanding of others that lived within the British Isles and the British Empire. This process greatly enriched our nation's history. The war was a terrible trial for the British people, but the victory of 1918 proves how great their courage and perseverance was. It is hard to imagine another generation able to endure the hardships and losses they did.

Glossary

Afrikanerdom – The concept of nationhood amongst Boers in South Africa.

Commando – Boer mounted military unit.

Democratisation – The increase of democratic rights in society.

Dilution of labour – The process whereby unskilled labourers replace skilled workers.

Franchise – The right to vote.

Gold standard – The support of a currency by gold reserves; for each banknote issued, there is a corresponding reserve of gold to the same value in the Treasury.

Home Rule, or **devolution** – Self-government within a larger polity such as the United Kingdom.

Imperial Preference – The encouragement to trade through free trade with specific states, in this case British colonies, but the imposition of tariffs on all 'foreign' goods.

Informal Empire – Economic influence exercised over a state without the formal administration of a colony.

Municipal socialism – Civic improvements designed to raise the quality of life of the majority.

Piece rate – Payment based on the quantity produced rather than on hours of work.

Protectorate – The extension of protection over a territory whilst avoiding interference in its own internal government. In practice, interference could be considerable.

Relative decline – Whilst an economy continues to grow, it fails to increase as quickly as other economies.

Sweated industry – Workers employed in piece rate and poor working conditions usually with low pay.

Syndicalism – The co-ordination of unions' strikes to force a government into concessions, including the general strike (a political weapon).

Uitlanders – Foreign workers in Transvaal (Afrikaans).

Universal suffrage – The concept where all have the right to vote.

Veldt – Field, the open countryside of South Africa.

Volksraad – The parliament of the Transvaal.

Bibliography and Further Reading

Hansard Parliamentary Debates (available in university libraries).
Paul Adelman, *The Rise of the Labour Party* (1972) Seminar Studies.
Paul Adelman, *Great Britain and the Irish Question, 1800–1922* (1996).
Robert Blake, *Disraeli* (1966).
George Boyce, *Nationalism in Ireland* (1982).
Sue Bruly, *Women in Britain since 1900* (1999).
Patrick Buckland, *Ulster Unionism* (Historical Association, 1973).
P.J. Cain and G. Hopkins, *British Imperialism*, I, (1993).
David Cannadine, *The Decline and Fall of the British Aristocracy* (1988).
M.E. Chamberlain, *Pax Britannica?* (1988).
John Charmley, *Splendid Isolation?* (1999).
George Dangerfield, *The Strange Death of Liberal England* (reprtd. 1987).
David Fitzpatrick, *The Two Irelands, 1912–1939* (1998).
R.F. Foster, *The Oxford Illustrated History of Ireland* (1991).
Morton Grenfell, *Home Rule and the Irish Question* (1999).
Eric Hobsbawm, *The Age of Empire* (1987).
Richard Holmes, *The Western Front* (2000).
Robert Johnson, *Studying History* (Studymates, 2000).
Stephen Lee, *Aspects of British Political History* (1994).
T.O. Lloyd, *Empire to Welfare State* (4th edn.1993).
Lyn MacDonald, *1914* (1987).
Lyn MacDonald, *Somme* (1983).
Arthur Marwick, *The Deluge* (1967).
Henry Pelling, *A History of British Trade Unionism* (1962).
Alan Palmer, *Dictionary of Modern History* (1962).
Martin Pugh, *Lloyd George* (1998).
Andrew Roberts, *Salisbury* (1999).
Robert Roberts, *The Classic Slum* (1971).
Keith Robbins, *The Eclipse of a Great Power* (1992).
L.C.B. Seaman, *Post-Victorian Britain* (1966).
Richard Shannon, *Gladstone* (1999).
Alan Sykes, *The Rise and Fall of British Liberalism, 1776–1985* (1997).
A.J.P. Taylor, *English History, 1914–1945* (1965).
Anthony Wood, *Nineteenth Century Britain* (2nd edn. 1982).

Web Sites for Students

Primary sources

www.pro.gov.uk
The excellent site of the Public Record Office which contains some articles on aspects of British history in this period.

www.fordham.edu/halsall/mod/modsbook.html
A huge site for modern historians including primary sources.

www.fordham/halsall/women/womensbook.html
Useful site for sources on women's history.

http://landow.stg.brown.edu/victorian/victor.html
Aspects of Victorian history.

Sites on British history

http://Britannica.com/bcom/history/0,5758,,00.html
This site will take you to more than just the whole Britannica encyclopaedia, and will focus on the historical aspects of personalties, events and by going to 'the web', there is access to 60 reviewed sites.

www.schoolzone.co.uk/resources/history_a-d.htm
Somewhat variable quality of this alphabetical list of sites.

www.about.com/arts/index.htm
Detailed sites on the nineteenth and twentieth centuries. Education: history is a section of 12 history collections. There are articles, chat areas and newsletters.

http://dir.yahoo.com/Arts?Humanities/history/
With 10,000 sites organised under period, people and places, this site has links to 300 sites on British history alone. Look up the Accrington Pals (a British unit in the Great War) which has a video of their fate on the Somme. There is also a link to an article called 'lions led by donkeys'.

www.ukans.edu/history/VL/
The University of Kansas maintains a virtual library but the quality varies and students of British history will only find some outline material useful for studying foreign policy.

www.ucr.edu/h-gig/horuslinks.html
H-GIG is part of the University of California and this site contains a vast list of historical sites but, again, only a few have direct relevance to British history.

http://search.msn.com/
MSN have a convenient search engine for specific searches but also a history site (Library: Humanities: History).

www.historytoday.com/historyreview/1298/main.stm
This excellent site contains articles, lists of contents, archives, students' notes and queries and lists of web sites. The *History Today* magazine itself is the host site with its own articles and archives. There is also History News, Notes and Queries, Web Site of the Week, and reviews.

www.spartakus.schoolnet.co.uk/Prparliament.htm
A range of material on parliamentary reform.

www.indiana.edu/~victoria/other.html
Links on British history between 1870 and 1901.

www.spartacus.schoolnet.co.uk/TU.htm
Links to sites on Labour and the trade union movement.

http://wwwvms.utexas.edu/~jdana/irehist.html
Ireland in the late nineteenth century is covered here.

http://britannia.com/bcom/internet -guide -display -page/1,5866,4504999,00.html
A list of British Prime Ministers and some articles on each of them.

http://history1700s.miningco.com/education/history1700s/msub38.htm
A site on the industrial revolution.

www.thehistorychannel.co.uk/index
The History Channel include a number of articles on the period covered in this book.

www.worldwar1.com/reflib.htm
The excellent and vast 'Trenches on the Web' site covering a great range of topics on the Great War.

www.westernfront.co.uk
The Western Front Association's site designed to 'remember' aspects of the Great War.

www.flyde.demon.co.uk/welcome.htm
A series of articles on the Western Front under the heading 'Hellfire Corner'.

www.hultongetty.com/en-us/HultonGetty/
An archive of thousands of images.

Book reviews

www.ihrinfo.ac.uk/ihr/reviews/revmnu.html
The Institute of Historical Research publish reviews of recent books on British history; a useful way to get an appraisal of historians' opinions.

Index

Afghanistan, 25–27, 44–46, 65, 69, 74–75, 117

Africa, 22, 27, 46, 49, 59, 64, 66–68, 70–73, 77–80, 124, 128
   (South Africa), 44, 49–50, 56, 59, 62, 66, 67, 71, 77–78, 79–80, 81, 85, 101, 117, 118, 124

agriculture, 21, 30–31, 41, 43, 48, 88, 93, 100, 137

America, 8, 17, 22, 26, 31, 33, 41, 48–49, 59, 63, 68, 89, 136, 139

Amiens, 140

aristocracy, 1, 3, 4–5, 13, 19, 50, 55, 140, 142

arms race, *see* Dreadnought

Askwith, George, 102, 103

Asquith, Herbert 87, 90, 95, 96, 105, 106, 113, 136, 140

Aubers Ridge, 126

Australia, 33, 54, 76, 101, 126–28

Balfour, Arthur, 34–35, 38, 50, 51, 56, 86

Balkans, 24, 25, 45, 65, 116, 120, 121

Beaconsfield, *see* Disraeli

Bechuanaland, 45, 49, 65

BEF (British Expeditionary Force), 124–125

Belgium, 17, 22, 65, 115, 120, 122, 124, 133

Boers, 27, 71, 77, 80

Bonar Law, Andrew, 106, 107–108, 137, 140, 144

Booth, Charles, 6, 88

Boyce, George, 131

Bridge, Admiral C., 61

Bright, John, 11, 75

Budget, 1909, 94

Burma, 73

Cain, P.J., and A.G. Hopkins, 70–71, 72

Campbell-Bannerman, Henry, 52, 87, 90, 94

Canada, 27, 54, 77, 117

Cannadine, David, 3

Cape Colony, 26, 50, 60, 69, 77

capitalism, 18, 70, 71, 80

Cardwell, Edward, 14, 15

Carson, Sir Edward, 37, 132

Cetewayo, 27

Chamberlain, Joseph, 5, 42, 45, 47, 48, 49, 56, 67, 78, 86, 116

Charmley, John, 64

China, 23, 49, 60, 62, 67, 69, 72, 75–76, 85, 116

Church, R.A., 8

Churchill, Randolph, 8, 33, 37, 51, 144

Churchill, Winston, 89, 92, 101, 113

City of London (the City), 9, 70–71, 72, 100

Coercion, Act, 33, 37

Coffee, King, 37

Coleman, Bruce, 28

Colenso, 79

Concert of Europe, 46, 61

Congress of Berlin, 25, 27

conscription, 129, 139

Conservativism, 11, 17, 19, 50–51, 55–56, 89

constitution, 2

Crimean War, 17, 23, 60, 69

Cyprus, 26

Dangerfield, George, 97, 108

Dartford speech, 52

Darwin, Charles, 13
Davison, Emily Wilding, 105
Defence of the Realm Act (DORA), 129
Derby, Lord (Earl Stanley), 12
Dillon, John, 34
Disraeli, Benjamin, 11, 16, 19, 20, 24, 25, 44, 51, 69, 71, 85
dockers, 7, 53, 102
Dreadnought, 84, 118–119
Dreikaiserbund, 23

Easter Rising, 131–132
Education, 5, 6, 13, 15, 21, 42, 43, 48, 52, 56, 76, 84, 91, 94, 104
Edward VII, 94, 95, 96, 116
Egypt, 22, 45–46, 60, 61, 65, 69
Entente Cordiale, 84, 116

Fabians, 110
Fashoda Incident, 67
Fenians, 32–33
Feuchtwanger, E.J., 14, 28
Forster, W.E., 14
France, 17, 22, 49, 62, 63, 64, 65, 67–68, 115, 120, 124, 133
Franco-Prussian War, 17, 24, 65
Free Trade, 11, 12–13, 41, 42, 49, 59, 86, 87
French, Sir John, 125, 132

Gallipoli, 126, 127
George V, 96, 107
Germany, 22, 26, 59, 64–65, 67, 75–76, 89, 92, 100, 117–118, 120, 121, 122, 140
Ghosh, P.R., 28
Gladstone, William Ewart, 11–12, 13, 14, 16, 17, 24, 25, 27–28
    Ireland, 32–38
    2nd Ministry, 42–47, 51
    Fourth Ministry, 53, 61
    later life, 69, 71, 97

Gleason, John, 23
Gordon, General Charles, 34, 46
Gorst, J.A., 19
Great Depression, 8, 22, 40
Grey, Sir Edward, 87, 104, 118, 122
Griffith, Arthur, 36, 139

Haig, Field Marshal Sir Douglas, 127, 132, 139
Hamer, D.A., 57
Harcourt, Sir William, 54
Hardie, Keir, 110, 111
Hawarden Kite, 34
Hobhouse, Emily, 80
Home Rule, 21, 33, 34–36, 37–38, 47–48, 52, 56, 92, 94, 95, 96, 97, 106–108, 139
Hong Kong, 67, 75
House of Lords Crisis, 93–96, 100.

Imperial Preference, *see* Tariff Reform
imperialism, 26–27, 44, 45, 47, 57, 68, 70, 71, 80, 85, 120
India, 22, 23, 24, 26, 44, 64, 67, 68, 69, 72, 73, 74, 75, 116, 127
Ireland, 2, 15, 21, 30–38, 42, 43, 51, 52, 53, 56, 83, 90, 130–132
Irish famine, 31
Italy, 45, 65, 72

Jameson Raid, 49, 78
Japan, 67, 75, 76, 81, 84, 115–116
Jenkins, T.A., 28
Jutland, Battle of, 128

Kennedy, Paul, 23, 60, 61, 62–63, 64
Kilmainham Treaty, 37
Kitchener, Field Marshal Lord, of Khartoum, 79, 85, 124, 125, 136
Kruger, Paul, 77, 78, 117

Labour Exchanges, 91–92, 112
Labour Party, and LRC, 86, 90, 92, 98,

104, 110–114, 143

Ladysmith, 79

Land War, 33, 52

Lansdowne, Lord, Fifth Marquis of, 76, 95, 116, 144

Leeds, C.A., 65

Liberalism, 12, 13–14, 47–48, 55–56, 87–88, 89, 97–98, 108–109, 129, 143

Liberal-Unionists, 34, 36, 47, 53, 56, 98

Licensing Act, 14, 56, 84, 94

Lloyd George, David, 4, 79, 87, 89–90, 94, 95, 102, 113, 119, 125, 129, 130, 132, 136–137, 139, 140, 144

Local Government, 53, 54, 93, 97

London, 1, 144

Loos, Battle of, 126

Lyons, F.S., 36

Lytton, Lord, First Earl of, 26

MacDonald, Ramsay, 111, 113

Mafeking, 79

Mahan, Alfred T., 63, 117

Majuba Hill, 27, 44, 72

Matthew, H.C.G., 28, 113

Mill, John Stuart, 13, 103

Milner, Sir Alfred, 78, 80

miners, 101–102

monarchy, 1–2, 18, 32, 97

Mons, 125

Morocco, 118

Municipal Socialism, 47

Near East, 23, 61

Newcastle Programme, 54, 97

New Zealand, 54, 76, 128

O'Brien, William, 34

O'Connell, Daniel, 32

O'Shea Scandal, 35–36

Ottoman Empire, 23, 24, 45, 66, 72, 117, 121

Pankhurst, Emmeline, 104–105

Parnell, Charles, 33, 34, 35–36

Pearse, Padraic, 130–131

Peel, Sir Robert, 12, 18, 19, 31, 32

Pensions, 48, 89, 90

Persia, 62, 69, 117

Phoenix Park Murders, 33

Plumer, General Sir Herbert, 137–138, 140

Plural voting, 56, 94, 96

Poison gas, 126, 129, 134

Poverty, 6–7, 15, 31, 43, 53, 87, 88, 89, 92, 93, 144

Pugh, Martin, 28, 105, 108

Redmond, John, 95, 96, 107, 130, 132

Rhodes, Cecil, 49, 71, 73, 77, 78

Rhodesia, 77

Roberts, Field Marshal Lord, of Kandahar, 27, 79, 84

Roberts, Robert, 7

Robinson R., and J. Gallagher, 70

Rosebery, Lord, 5th Earl of, 54, 57, 98

Royal Navy, 1, 25, 51, 54, 59–62, 64–65, 67, 84, 88, 117, 120, 128

Russell, Lord John, 12, 23

Russia, 17, 23-7, 44, 46, 62, 64–67, 74–76, 115, 120–122, 136, 139

Salisbury, Robert Cecil, 3rd Marquis, 26, 33, 50–52, 59, 64, 66, 68, 81, 144

Saul, S.B., 8–9, 40

Self Help, 13, 18, 50, 53, 87

Shannon, Richard, 28

Shell Shortage Scandal, 126

Sierra Leone, 49

Singapore, 73

Sinn Fein, 36, 38, 132, 139

Social Democratic Federation, 87, 110, 112

Somme, Battle of the, 132–135, 138, 139

Smuts, Jan, 79, 128

Steel, 8–9, 118

Suez Canal, 22, 24, 45, 61, 116
Suffragettes, 93, 100, 103–106
Syndicalism, 100, 102

Taff Vale, 84–85, 87, 90, 103
Tariff Reform, 49–50, 56, 86, 87
Tanks, 129, 134, 138, 140
Taylor, A.J.P., 16, 136
Taylor, Robert, 64
Trade Unions 11, 14–15, 53, 55, 90, 93, 100, 110–111, 130
Transvaal, 27, 44, 49–50, 70, 71, 72, 77–78, 118
Trusts, 41

Uganda, 49, 65, 71, 73
Uitlanders, 78
Ulster and Unionism, 30–31, 32, 36–37, 38, 100, 106–108

Unauthorised Programme, 47–48
United States of America, *see* America
Universities, 14, 42

de Valera, Eamonnn, 130, 132, 139
Victoria, 1, 21
Vincent, John, 28

Wei Hei Wei, 49, 67, 76
Wilson, Trevor, 108
Wolseley, General Sir Garnet, 46, 49, 71
Women, 42, 52, 53, 54, 76, 79, 103–106, 140, 144
WSPU, *see* Suffragettes

Ypres, Battles of, 125, 136, 138, 139

Zulu War, 27